Railways Restored 1980

LONDON
IAN ALLAN LTD

First published 1980

ISBN 0 7110 1033 1

Published by Ian Allan Ltd, Shepperton, Surrey; and printed by Ian Allan Printing Ltd at their works at Coombelands in Runnymede, England

Cover: ***Ex-SR 'S15' class 4-6-0 No 841*** **Greene King** ***seen in action on the North Yorkshire Moors Railway in September 1979.***
W. A. Sharman

Title page: ***Class '2' 2-6-0 No 46464 leaves Boat of Garten.*** *Strathspey Railway*

Below: Members of the Great Western Society tackle a track-laying job at Didcot Railway Centre.
Great Western Society

The publishers, the railway operators and the Association of Railway Preservation Societies accept no liability for any loss, damage or injury caused by error or inaccuracy in the information or timetables published in *Railways Restored 1980*. Train services may be altered or cancelled without prior notice, and at some locations diesel traction may be substituted for scheduled steam workings.

Contents

Above: ***Ex-GWR '1400' class 0-4-2T No 1450 nears Buckfastleigh with the 16.10 from Totnes Riverside on 5 September 1979.*** *M. S. Wilkins*

The Association of Railway Preservation Societies

The ARPS and *Railways Restored*

The Association of Railway Preservation Societies (ARPS) is delighted to hand over the editing and production of its annual year book to Ian Allan Ltd under its new title *Railways Restored* and in an entirely new form.

We were very proud of our previous *Steam* year books and wish this publication every success — any reputable book that gives accurate publicity to our members is welcome and will receive our support.

The raison d'être of railway preservation is more than merely 'pickling' locomotives and carriages. In the past, various museums, partly or wholly devoted to railways, did an excellent job in caring for retired locomotives, carriages and other paraphernalia — but such exhibits often seemed dormant if not dead. Railway preservation societies, on the other hand, aim to maintain steam railway equipment not only in good-looking condition, but, where possible, in first-class mechanical order and this practice has now been followed by the National Railway Museum at York.

In the workshops of preserved railways and steam centres, and at York, some steam locomotives and carriages are maintained to the standards required for excursions over main lines. For such trains, British Rail quite properly demand high standards of maintenance. Elsewhere whole railways have been acquired and are operated to standards required by the Department of Transport. These lines pay their way — and profits are ploughed back. Personal remuneration is kept to a minimum.

Through the efforts of railway preservation societies an extensive range of railway items, covering almost the whole spectrum of the age of steam railways, is being preserved. Without the efforts of these enthusiasts, steam trains would now be known only through pictures, recordings, models — and memories.

Railway preservation societies have tended to spring up independently, through the initiative of their promoters. But all such societies have interests in common. New societies benefit from access to the know-how of established societies. Established societies, for their part, find it in their interest that new ones should be soundly organised, to minimise the possibility of physical or financial disaster, which would mar the whole movement in the public eye. All societies benefit from information about sources of equipment and material. They benefit, too, from joint publicity and from joint representation to other national bodies.

These needs are met by the Association of Railway Preservation Societies Ltd. Most railway preservation societies in the British Isles are members of the Association which is a non-profit-distributing voluntary body, incorporated as a company limited by guarantee.

Background of ARPS

The Association originated in the early 1960s largely due to the efforts of the late Mr Noel Draycott who united five preservation groups under the banner of the Railway Preservation Society and laid the keel of the ARPS.

Today it has 64 member societies (full members and 64 associate members) — there are also over 500 private members.

The ARPS has always maintained very close liaison with British Railways and one of the first major events in our history occurred on 1 April 1962 with the running of the 'Blue Belle', hauled by Captain Bill Smith's GN 'J52' 0-6-0ST No 1247 from London Bridge to Sheffield Park and return. Dr Beeching joined the train at Three Bridges and on arrival at Sheffield Park said: 'In order to make the whole system of British Railways more healthy and vigorous, it will be necessary to displace some of the old equipment and some services.

'As we do that, so the desirability of preservation will become more apparent, but I would like to warn all those people who are interested in it that you must not overdo it to the point where you spoil the market for yourselves. I think, in this connection, the setting up of the Association of Railway Preservation Societies is likely to be a very helpful measure because we can well afford to have a scattering of preservation societies throughout the country, but if it is done to excess, then the efforts of those who are most serious will be spoiled by those who are not prepared to put in enough effort to run societies properly.'

ARPS and its objects

The principal objects of the Association are to further the mutual co-operation of railway preservation organisations, to promote publicity on their behalf and to encourage high standards of competence.

Also, to maintain close contact with other railway preservation bodies such as the Association of Minor Railway Companies, British Rail, the British Tourist Authority, the Department of Education and Science, the Transport Trust, the Consultative Panel for the Preservation of British Transport Relics and the Friends of the National Railway Museum at York.

There are three things the Association does not do: it runs no railway preservation activities directly itself; and it neither raises funds nor distributes them. Subscriptions cover only running expenses.

By encouraging high standards the Association safeguards the interests of the public who visit and subscribe to railway preservation schemes. Full membership is not granted lightly, and Full Members must give an assurance that they will comply with the Association's Code of Practice. Points covered by the code include proper constitutions and accounts, comprehensive insurance cover, limited liability for people belonging to groups which operate railways, safe operation, and administration by adults. Applicants for membership which fall short of fulfilling all the Code's requirements, but which nevertheless appear responsible, are eligible to be admitted as Associate Members, and individuals who support the objects of the association may join as Private Members. An advantage of these lower grades of membership is to give promoters of preservation schemes access to the Association's advice at an early stage, when they most need it.

Advice is freely available to members from the Association's advisers, specialists who also have experience of railway preservation. Subjects with which they deal include accounts, insurance, mechanical engineering, railway operating, and many others.

Information sheets are published for members. Subjects covered range from the form of agreement for the use of privately-owned locomotives on operating railways, through charitable status and rates for film-making, to value added tax and safety. Further advisers and information sheets are likely to be added from time to time.

Meetings are held three times a year, usually on member railways or at their depots, and enable members' representatives to meet formally and informally, and to inspect the preservation activities of their hosts.

The mainstay of the ARPS is its newsletter, produced normally once a month. This gives information on availability of locomotives, rolling stock and relics for preservation, with notes on progress made by member organisations. The Association acts as a clearing house, matching relics to society.

An arbitration service is available in the event of a dispute between members.

The achievements of the Association include:

—Block purchases of steam locomotives at reasonable prices, negotiated with British Rail on behalf of member societies.
—The release was negotiated, from the scrapyard of Woodham Bros, Barry, of the first of many steam locomotives which had been disposed of by BR on condition that they would not be re-sold.
—Arrangements made for locomotives and other exhibits from the National Collection to be taken on loan by members (eg: *Oliver Cromwell* at Bressingham, the 'Q1' at Bluebell etc).
—When steam locomotives were banned from British Rail, a successful 'Return to Steam' campaign was mounted.
—The yearly publication of the 'yellow' *Guide to Steam Trains* leaflet issued free to the public and with a distribution of 200,000 copies.
—The organisation and administration in 1978 of the first ever Railway Preservation Symposium, in conjunction with its sister bodies. Held at the Institution of Civil Engineers with a full house and chaired by the Director of the Science Museum, Dame Margaret Weston DBE, and the BR Board Member for Operations, Mr James Urquhart, the symposium certainly marked the Association's coming of age.

'How long can it all go on? — surely the bubble will burst,' sing the Jonahs! To both the questions the ARPS has a firm answer — for ever and no.

But it will require even greater strength and determination in united effort.

Probably the greatest problem is that of the future maintenance and repair of locomotives and this has top priority — the human skills still exist and strenuous and united efforts are being made to preserve these and to train younger personnel before it is too late. More workshops and more workshop volunteers are the concern of today's preservationists. (see page 88 for details of how to join the ARPS).

1980 — A Great Railway Year

The ARPS will be closely associated with the following events during 1980:

5 May
150th Anniversary of the Canterbury and Whitstable Railway and the return of *Invicta* to Canterbury. For further details apply to: The Curator, Royal Museum, High Street, Canterbury, Kent CT1 2JE.

24, 25, 26 May
Rocket 150, Steam-past at Rainhill. For further details apply to: Tony Quirke, Rocket 150, British Rail, Rail House, Lord Nelson Street, Liverpool L1 1JF.

August
20th Anniversary of Bluebell Railway. Apply to Bluebell Railway, Sheffield Park, Uckfield, Sussex.

Saturday 13 September
Railway Preservation Convention at Renold Theatre Manchester, University of Manchester Institute of Science and Technology. Guest of Honour: Dame Margaret Weston, DBE; Director of the Science Museum. For further details, apply to: David Sumner, Festival Administrator, PO Box 430, County Hall, Piccadilly Gardens, Manchester M60 3HP.

Sunday 14 September
Conclusion of Liverpool/Manchester Railway Celebrations: The Rainhill Anniversary train run.

So, we are delighted to be able to launch our first year book under the baton of Ian Allan Ltd in league with an exciting programme for 1980.

Capt Peter F. Manisty, RN (Retd) Chairman,
The Association of Railway Preservation Societies

ARPS Annual Award

This is made to a member Group making an outstanding contribution to voluntary railway preservation during the year of the Award.

Previous awards have been made to:

1975—the Great Western Society Ltd
1976—the Princess Elizabeth Locomotive Society
1977—the Peterborough Railway Society Ltd (Nene Valley Railway)
1978—the Festiniog Railway Society

The Award consists of a coat of arms, on loan from the National Railway Museum. It is of cast metal painted in full colour and was used to adorn a royal train locomotive, although its origins are obscure.

The 1979 award goes to the Severn Valley Railway Co Ltd for its outstanding contribution to railway preservation in restoring to working order, or providing facilities for the restoration of, five steam locomotives: GWR Nos 2857, 4930 *Hagley Hall*, 5164, and 7812 *Erlestoke Manor*, and LMS No 5000. Four of these five locomotives had been recovered from Woodham Bros scrapyard at Barry and two of them (4930 from Barry and 5000 from the National Collection) were passed to run on British Rail.

In reaching this conclusion the award sub-committee considered several other worthy candidates and in this instance departs from its usual practice by publicly recognising the achievement of members of the Mid-Hants RPS and others in the restoration to working order of SR No 34016 *Bodmin*, also recovered from Barry.

Left: ***Two of the locomotives for which the Severn Valley received the ARPS award. GW 'Hall' 4-6-0 No 4930*** **Hagley Hall** ***and LMS '5MT' 4-6-0 No 5000 storm away from Shrewsbury with the 'Inter-City' tour on 22 September 1979.*** *M. S. Wilkins*

Preserved Railways and Preservation Centres

On the following pages will be found a guide to the major preserved railways, railway museums and preservation centres in the British Isles. Information for visitors has been set out in tabular form for easy reference, together with a complete locomotive stocklist for each centre. The geographical location of each line or centre is indicated on the map opposite by the appropriate page number. *Railways Restored* includes a section giving timetable details of some of the operating lines, but some lines were unable to submit their timetables in time for inclusion.

Many preservation centres and operating lines provide facilities for other groups and organisations to restore locomotives and equipment on their premises. It has not been possible to include full details of these groups, but organisations which own locomotives are shown under the centres at which they operate. In addition a full list of member societies of the ARPS is given on page 81.

Due to 'Rocket 150' at Rainhill in May a number of locomotives listed under preservation centres may be absent from their usual home base during the period.

Chris Leigh
Alan Butcher

Abbreviations

AEC	Associated Equipment Company
A/Barclay	Andrew Barclay & Sons
A/Porter	Aveling and Porter Ltd
B/Peacock	Beyer Peacock & Co
B/Hawthorn	Black, Hawthorn & Co
BTH	British Thomson Houston
D/Metcalfe	Davies and Metcalfe
E/Electric	English Electric Ltd
F/Jennings	Fletcher Jennings & Co
F/Walker	Fox Walker
G/England	George England & Co
H/Clarke	Hudswell Clarke & Co Ltd
H/Leslie	Hawthorn Leslie & Co
K/Stuart	Kerr Stuart & Co Ltd
M/Rail	Motorail
M/Vick	Metrovick
M/Wardle	Manning Wardle & Co Ltd
O&K	Orenstein & Koppel
RSH	Robert Stephenson & Hawthorn Ltd
R/Hornsby	Ruston Hornsby
4w	4-wheel
D	Diesel
DH	Diesel-hydraulic
DM	Diesel-mechanical
E	Electric
F	Fireless
G	Geared
P	Petrol
PM	Petrol-mechanical
PT	Pannier tank
ST	Saddle tank
T	Side tanks
VB	Vertical boiler

Late Information

Peveril ex-IoM acquired by National Railway Museum
Jessie (Hunslet (1873/37) acquired by Norchard Steam Centre
35018 *British India Line* acquired by Mid-Hants Railway
31625 acquired by Mid-Hants Railway
D5705 acquired by Diesel Traction Group
D1015 *Western Champion* acquired by Diesel Traction Group
740 Danish S class 2-6-4T acquired by Nene Valley Railway
69023 *Joem* offered for sale
3.628 SNCF 230D class offered for sale by the Nord Locomotive Preservation Group
W79978 offered for sale by North Yorkshire Moors Railway

NORTH SEA
IRISH SEA
ENGLISH CHANNEL
INVERNESS
74 AVIEMORE
ABERDEEN
PERTH
LOCHTY 75
76 FALKIRK
77
GLASGOW
EDINBURGH
NEWCASTLE
BEAMISH 71
CARLISLE
BOWES 73
78
LARNE
79
BELFAST
DARLINGTON 71
WHITBY
63
57 RAVENGLASS
56 ULVERSTON
79 DOUGLAS
59 CARNFORTH
73 EMBSAY
66 YORK
KEIGHLEY 61
LEEDS
64
HULL
SOUTHPORT 60
60 BURY
DONCASTER
LIVERPOOL
MANCHESTER
DUBLIN
58 DINTING
HOLYHEAD
40 PENRHYN
SNOWDON
35
34 LLANBERIS
CREWE
48
49
SHERINGHAM
42
31 LLANGOLLEN
STOKE
DERBY
39 PORTMADOC
40 OSWESTRY
52 STAFFORD
44 LOUGHBOROUGH
BALA 33
BROWNHILLS
NORWICH
SHREWSBURY
LEICESTER
TYWYN 36
38 WELSHPOOL
PETERBOROUGH
43
45 SHACKERSTONE
BIRMINGHAM
FAIRBOURNE 34
55
50
BRESSINGHAM 46
ABERYSTWYTH 37
53
BRIDGNORTH
ROSSLARE
CAMBRIDGE
54
15 LEIGHTON BUZZARD
47
FISHGUARD
45
17 QUAINTON RD
26
GLOUCESTER
31 CARMARTHEN
CAERPHILLY 41
26
18 DIDCOT
20
30 SWINDON
LONDON
CARDIFF
SWANSEA
26
BRISTOL
15 SITTINGBOURNE
19
23
24
TENTERDEN 12
14 ALTON
10 SHEFFIELD PARK
16 HYTHE
TAUNTON
SOUTHAMPTON
BRIGHTON
PORTSMOUTH
13
EXETER
27 SWANAGE
TOTNES
22
PLYMOUTH
21 KINGSWEAR

SOUTH-EAST

Bluebell Railway

Headquarters: Bluebell Railway Preservation Society, Sheffield Park station, Uckfield, East Sussex TN22 3QL
Telephone: Newick 2370
Main station: Sheffield Park
Other public stations: Horsted Keynes
Car parks: Sheffield Park, Horsted Keynes
Access by public transport: Haywards Heath BR and bus to Horsted Keynes village, or direct to Sheffield Park in summer
Refreshment facilities: Sheffield Park, Horsted Keynes
Souvenir shops: Sheffield Park, Horsted Keynes
Museum: Sheffield Park
Depots: Sheffield Park (locomotives), Horsted Keynes (stock)
Passenger trains: Sheffield Park-Horsted Keynes (5 miles)
Period of public operation: Sundays in January, February and December, also Boxing and New Year's Day. Saturdays and Sundays in March, April and November. Wednesdays, Saturdays and Sundays in May and October. Daily in June-September inclusive. Open for limited viewing at other times
Special notes: Vintage and special weekends are held during the year

Locomotives

Name	*No*	*Origin*	*Class*	*Type*	*Built*
—	27	SECR	P	0-6-0T	1910
—	55	LBSCR	A1X	0-6-0T	1875
Fenchurch	72	LBSCR	A1X	0-6-0T	1872
Pioneer II	178	SECR	P	0-6-0T	1910
Bluebell	323	SECR	P	0-6-0T	1910
—	263	SECR	H	0-4-4T	1905
Birch Grove	473	LBSCR	E4	0-6-2T	1898
—	488	LSWR	0415	4-4-2T	1885
—	592	SECR	C	0-6-0	1901
—	2650	NLR		0-6-0T	1880
—	9017	GWR	9000	4-4-0	1938
—	30064	SR	USA	0-6-0T	1943
—	33001	SR	Q1	0-6-0	1942
—	30541	SR	Q	0-6-0	1939
—	30847	SR	S15	4-6-0	1937
—	1618	SR	U	2-6-0	1928
—	30096	LSWR	B4	0-4-0T	1905
Sir Archibald Sinclair	34059	SR	BB	4-6-2	1947
Camelot	73082	BR	5MT	4-6-0	1955
—	75027	BR	4MT	4-6-0	1954
—	80100	BR	4MT	2-6-4T	1954
—	92240	BR	9F	2-10-0	1959
Blackmore Vale	21C123	SR	WC	4-6-2	1946

Industrial locomotives

Name	*No*	*Builder*	*Type*	*Built*
Blue Circle	—	A/Porter (9449)	2-2-0TG	1926
Baxter	—	F/Jennings (158)	0-4-0T	1877
Stamford	—	Avonside (1972)	0-6-0ST	1927

Below:** The Bulleid Society's restored 4-6-2 No 21C123* **Blackmore Vale** ***heads a Bluebell Railway afternoon train away from Sheffield Park. *John Titlow*

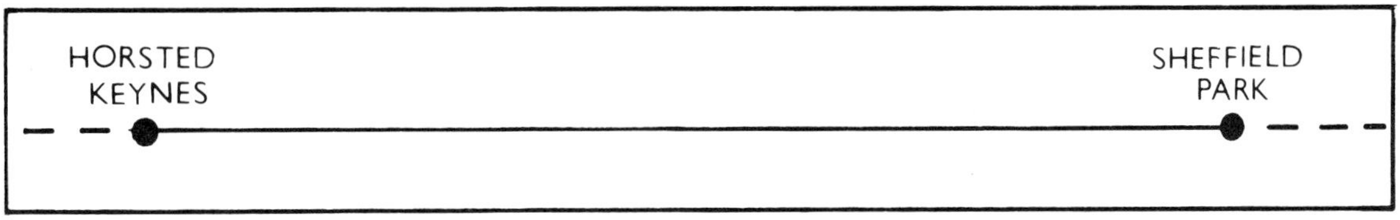

Stock

Substantial collection of pre-Nationalisation coaches including SECR, Bulleid, Maunsell and Chesham vehicles. Also freight stock

Above: ***During one of the railway's 'Bluebell on Parade' days the Maunsell Locomotive Society's 'U' Class 2-6-0 No 1618 climbs Freshfield bank with a short freight train.***
P. H. Groom

Owners

592 (the Wainwright C Class Preservation Society)
30064 (the Southern Locomotive Preservation Society)
1618 (the Maunsell Locomotive Society Ltd)
30541 (the Maunsell Locomotive Society Ltd)
30847 (the Maunsell Locomotive Society Ltd)
30096 (the Bulleid Society Ltd)
21C123 (the Bulleid Society Ltd)
263 (the H Class Trust)
73082 (the Camelot Locomotive Society)
33001 (on loan from the National Railway Museum)

Kent & East Sussex Railway

Headquarters: Tenterden Railway Co Ltd, Tenterden Town station, Tenterden, Kent TN30 6HE
Telephone: Tenterden 2943
Main station: Tenterden Town
Other public stations: Rolvenden, Wittersham Road
Car parks: Tenterden, Wittersham Road
Access by public transport: Maidstone & District bus service No 400 from Ashford (Kent) BR station
Refreshment facilities: Tenterden Town. Also on train facilities
Souvenir shop: Tenterden Town station
Museum: Station Road, Tenterden
Depot: Rolvenden
Passenger trains: Tenterden-Wittersham Road (4 miles). Hourly 11.00-17.00 on Bank Holidays. Otherwise 12.00(SX), 14.00, 15.15 and 16.30 from Tenterden
Period of public operation: Weekends and Bank Holidays from Easter to December. Daily from 12 July-31 August
Special notes: 'Wealden Pullman' dining car service operates on Saturday evenings. Advance booking is essential for this train

Locomotives

Name	*No*	*Origin*	*Class*	*Type*	*Built*
Bodiam	3	LBSCR	A1X	0-6-0T	1872
Sutton	10	LBSCR	A1X	0-6-0T	1876
Pride of Sussex	11	SECR	P	0-6-0T	1909
Wainwright	21	SR	USA	0-6-0T	1943
Maunsell	22	SR	USA	0-6-0T	1943
—	20	GWR	AEC	diesel railcar	1940

Industrial locomotives

Name	*No*	*Builder*	*Type*	*Built*
—	16	BTH	Bo-Bo	1932
Arthur	17	M/Wardle (1601)	0-6-0ST	1903
Westminster	18	Peckett (1378)	0-6-0ST	1914
Holman F. Stephens	23	Hunslet (3791)	0-6-0ST	1952
William H. Austen	24	Hunslet (3800)	0-6-0ST	1953
Linda	—	Hunslet (3781)	0-6-0ST	1952
Sapper	97	Hunslet (3797)	0-6-0ST	1953
Dolobran	38	M/Wardle (1762)	0-6-0ST	1910
Rhyl	41	M/Wardle (2009)	0-6-0ST	1921
—	26	RSH (7667)	0-6-0ST	1950
Gervase	—	M/Wardle (1472)	0-4-0TG	1900
Minnie	—	F/Walker (385)	0-6-0ST	1878
Baglan	27	E/Electric	0-4-0DH	1962
—	28	Hunslet (4208)	0-6-0DM	1948

Stock
3 ex-SECR 'Birdcage' coaches
7 ex-SR coaches
2 1926-built Pullman cars
3 ex-BR Mk1 coaches
Small number of miscellaneous freight vehicles

Owners
10 (Sutton Borough Council)

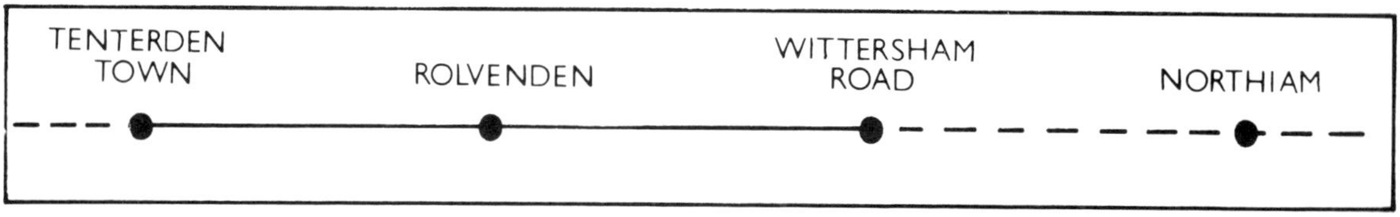

Below: ***'Terrier' 0-6-0T No 10*** **Sutton** ***arrives at Rolvenden on the Kent & East Sussex Railway with a train from Tenterden.***
B. Morrison

Isle of Wight Steam Railway

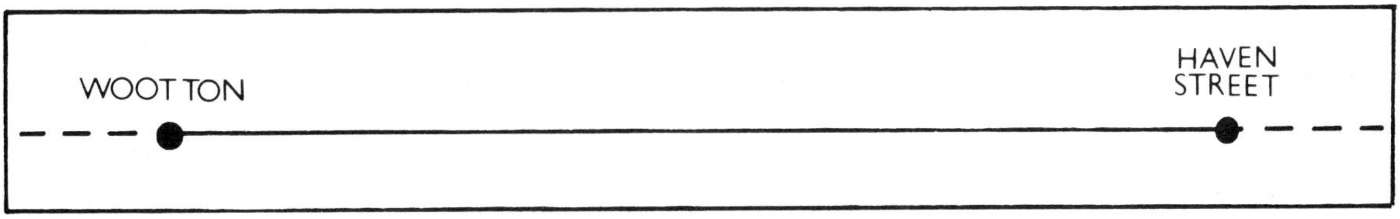

Headquarters: Isle of Wight Steam Railway, Haven Street station, Ryde, Isle of Wight PO33 4DS
Main station: Haven Street
Car park: Haven Street
Access by public transport: Southern Vectis bus services Nos 3/43 from Ryde, (connecting with ferries from Portsmouth) and Newport
Refreshment facilities: Light refreshments available
Souvenir shop: Haven Street
Museum: Small exhibits museum at Haven Street
Depot: Haven Street
Passenger trains: Haven Street-Wootton (2 miles)
Period of public operation: Sundays Easter then May-September. Thursdays July and August. Daily week before August Bank Holiday. Bank Holiday Mondays, Easter, May, Spring, August
Special notes: Summer Steam Show, August Bank Holiday Saturday, Sunday and Monday. Traction Engines, Fairground Organs, Vintage Cars, etc

Locomotives

Name	*No*	*Origin*	*Class*	*Type*	*Built*
Freshwater	W8	LBSCR	A1X	0-6-0T	1876
—	W11	LBSCR	A1X	0-6-0T	1878
Calbourne	W24	LSWR	02	0-4-4T	1891

Industrial locomotives

Name	*No*	*Builder*	*Type*	*Built*
Vectis	37	H/Leslie (3135)	0-4-0ST	1915
Ajax	38	Barclay (1605)	0-6-0T	1918
Spitfire	39	R/Hornsby (242868)	4wDM	1916

Stock

3 IWR coaches (bodies only)
3 LBSCR coaches
3 SECR coaches
1 LCDR coach (body only)
1 crane
1 ex-BR ballast tamper
1 Wickham trolley
21 wagons

Above: ***The sole survivor of its type, Class '02' 0-4-4T No 24*** **Calbourne** ***drifts into Haven Street on the Isle of Wight steam Railway.*** *P. Relf*

Mid-Hants Railway

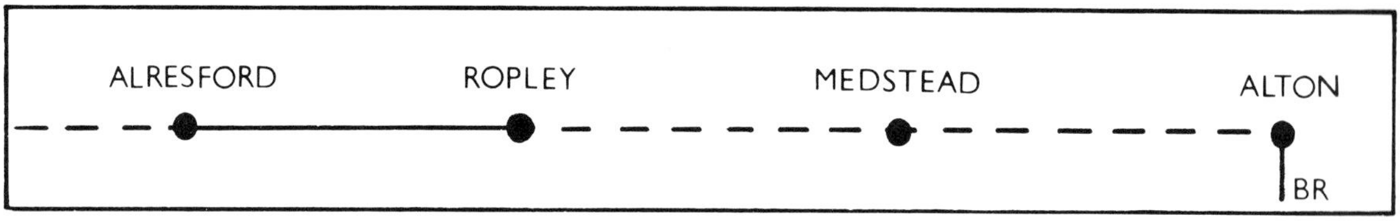

Headquarters: Winchester & Alton Railway Ltd, Alresford station, Alresford, Hants SO24 9JG
Telephone: Alresford 3810
Main station: Alresford
Other public stations: Ropley
Car park: Alresford
Access by public transport: Winchester and Alton BR stations, Alder Valley/Hants & Dorset bus services Nos 214 and X14 (weekdays), Alder Valley bus service No 452 (Sundays)
Refreshment facilities: Alresford
Souvenir shops: Alresford, Ropley
Depot: Ropley
Passenger trains: Alresford-Ropley (3 miles). Saturday 13.00-17.00 (45min interval), Sunday 11.00-18.00 (30min interval — during peak season)
Period of public operation: Weekends and Bank Holidays from end of March-October

Above: *After long and painstaking restoration, Bulleid light Pacific No 34016* Bodmin *was returned to traffic on the Mid-Hants Railway during September 1979.* *David Eatwell*

Locomotives

Name	*No*	*Origin*	*Class*	*Type*	*Built*
—	30506	LSWR	S15	4-6-0	1920
—	31806	SR	U	2-6-0	1926
—	31874	SR	N	2-6-0	1925
Bodmin	34016	SR	WC	4-6-2	1945
Swanage	34105	SR	WC	4-6-2	1950
—	47324	LMS	3F	0-6-0T	1926
—	76017	BR	4MT	2-6-0	1954

Industrial locomotives

Name	*No*	*Builder*	*Type*	*Built*
—	2	Bagnall (2842)	0-4-0ST	1946
—	3	H/Clarke (1544)	0-6-0ST	1924
—	4	Fowler (22889)	0-4-0DM	1939
Errol Lonsdale	196	Hunslet (3796)	0-6-0ST	1953

Stock
2 steam cranes
1 'Plassermatic' tamping/levelling machine
13 ex-BR Mk1 coaches
8 ex-SR coaches
3 ex-LSWR coaches
Numerous goods vehicles

Owners
3 (Slough Estates)
506 (the Urie S15 Locomotive Preservation Group)
34105 (the 34105 Light Pacific Group)
47324 (the Fowler 3F Preservation Society)
76017 (the Standard 4 Locomotive Group)

Sittingbourne and Kemsley Light Railway

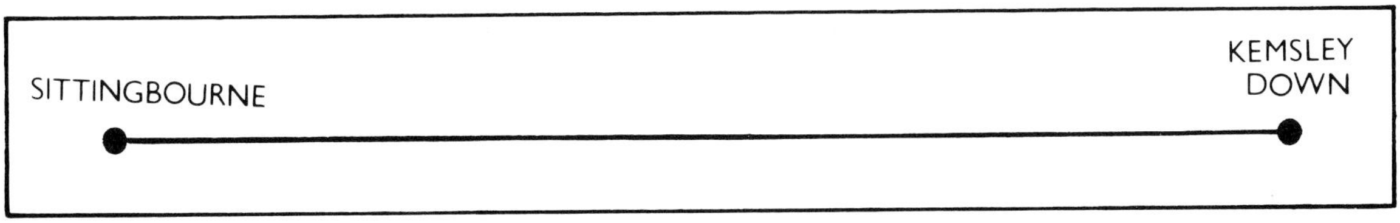

Headquarters: Sittingbourne & Kemsley Light Railway Ltd, Milton Road, Sittingbourne, Kent
Telephone: Sittingbourne 24899 (operating times only)
Main station: Sittingbourne
Car park: Sittingbourne
Access by public transport: Sittingbourne BR station, A2 and M2 roads
Refreshment facilities: Sittingbourne, Kemsley Down
Souvenir shops: Sittingbourne, Kemsley Down
Depot: Kemsley Down (access by rail only)
Passenger trains: 2ft 6in gauge ex-industrial line Sittingbourne-Kemsley Down (2 miles)
Period of public operation: Weekends and Bank Holidays April-October. Tuesdays, Wednesdays, Thursdays during August.
Special notes: There is no public access to Kemsley Down other than by the railway on operating dates. When the line is closed all stock is stored in security compounds, on the mill premises

Locomotives

Name	*No*	*Builder*	*Type*	*Built*
Alpha	—	Bagnall (2472)	0-6-2T	1932
Triumph	—	Bagnall (2511)	0-6-2T	1934
Superb	—	Bagnall (2624)	0-6-2T	1940
Unique	—	Bagnall (2216)	2-4-0F	1924
Premier	—	K/Stuart (886)	0-4-2ST	1905
Leader	—	K/Stuart (926)	0-4-2ST	1905
Melior	—	K/Stuart (4219)	0-4-2ST	1924
Edward Lloyd	—	R/Hornsby (435403)	4wDM	1961
Victor	—	Hunslet (614)	4wDM	1896

Industrial standard gauge locomotives

Name	*No*	*Builder*	*Type*	*Built*
Swanscombe	—	H/Leslie (3718)	0-4-0ST	1928
Bear	—	Peckett (614)	0-4-0ST	1896
	—	A/Barclay (1876)	0-4-0F	1925

Stock
10 bogie coaches (4 ex-Chattenden & Upnor Railway)
2 open coaches
33 pulp wagons
20 other wagons

Leighton Buzzard Narrow Gauge Railway

Headquarters: Leighton Buzzard Narrow Gauge Rly, Page's Park station, Billington Road, Leighton Buzzard LU7 8TN
Telephone: (0525) 373888
Main station: Pages Park, (Billington Road, Leighton Buzzard)
Other public stations: Halts at Stanbridge Road, Leedon and Vandyke Junction
Car park: Pages Park
Access by public transport: Leighton Buzzard BR station then by bus to town centre
Refreshment facilities: Pages Park
Souvenir shop: Pages Park
Depots: Pages Park and Stonehenge Works
Passenger trains: 2ft gauge line Pages Park-Vandyke Junction ($1\frac{1}{2}$ miles)
Period of public operation: Sundays April-September and Bank Holiday Mondays and Saturdays (except Christmas)

Locomotives

Name	*No*	*Builder*	*Type*	*Built*
Chaloner	1*	de Winton	0-4-0VBT	1877
Pixie	2	K/Stuart (4260)	0-4-0ST	1922
Rishra	3	Baguley (2007)	0-4-0T	1921
The Doll	4	Barclay (1641)	0-6-0T	1919
Pam	7	O&K (8986)	4wDM	1939
Elf	5	O&K (12740)	0-6-0WT	1936
Haydn Taylor	10	Simplex (7956)	4wDM	1945
P. C. Allen	11	O&K (5834)	0-4-0WT	1912
Carbon	12	Simplex (6012)	4wDM	1930
Caravan	6	Simplex (7192)	4wDM	1938
	14	Hunslet (3646)	4wDM	1946
	15	Planet (2514)	4wDM	1935
Gandelf	16	Lister (11221)	4wDM	1939
	43	Simplex (10409)	4wDM	1954
	44	Simplex (7933)	4wDM	1941

*No 1 is on loan to the National Railway Museum, York until 1981

Stock
7 coaches and a number of miscellaneous vehicles

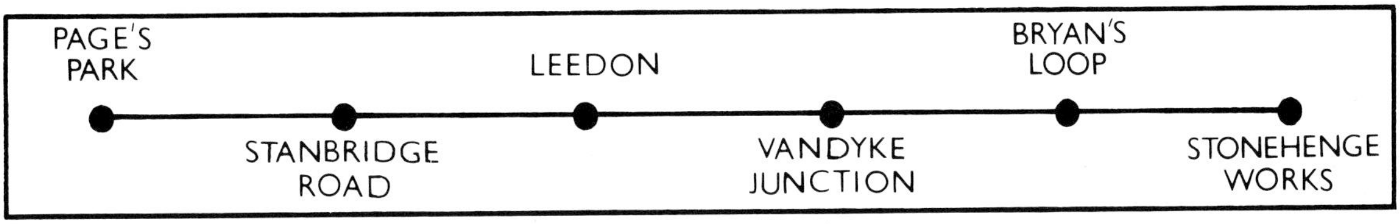

Romney, Hythe and Dymchurch Railway

Headquarters: Romney Hythe and Dymchurch Railway, New Romney station, Kent
Telephone: New Romney 2353
Main station: New Romney
Other public stations: Hythe, Dymchurch, St Mary's Bay, Greatstone, Maddieson's, Lade, The Pilot, Dungeness
Car parks: Hythe, Dymchurch, New Romney, Dungeness
Access by public transport: Sandling Junction BR station (1½ miles), Folkestone Central BR station — 4 miles: bus connection
Refreshment facilities: New Romney, Dungeness
Souvenir shops: Hythe, New Romney
Museum: New Romney
Depot: New Romney
Passenger trains: 15in gauge line. Train frequency depends on the time of year: (maximum frequency is 30 minutes Hythe — New Romney, 60 minutes New Romney — Dungeness)
Period of public operation: Daily March-September. Weekends February, October, November
Special notes: Cheap return fares are available on Friday mornings. Model railway and exhibition at New Romney. Parties can be catered for at New Romney

Locomotives

Name	*No*	*Builder*	*Type*	*Built*
Green Goddess	1	Davey Paxman	4-6-2	1925
Northern Chief	2	Davey Paxman	4-6-2	1925
Southern Maid	3	Davey Paxman	4-6-2	1926
The Bug	4	Krauss	0-4-0T	1926
Hercules	5	Davey Paxman	4-8-2	1926
Samson	6	Davey Paxman	4-8-2	1926
Typhoon	7	Davey Paxman	4-6-2	1926
Hurricane	8	Davey Paxman	4-6-2	1926
Winston Churchill	9	YEC	4-6-2	1931
Doctor Syn	10	YEC	4-6-2	1931
Black Prince	11	Krupps	4-6-2	1937
	PW1	M/Rail (7059)	4wDM	1938
	PW2	RH&DR	4wPM	1965
Redgauntlet	PW3	RH&DR	4wPM	1975

Stock

45 bogie coaches
14 open bogie coaches
3 semi-open coaches
40 assorted wagons

Below: *RHDR 4-6-2* **Northern Chief** *stands at New Romney shed, looking a good deal younger than its 54 years on 16 July 1979.* A. H. Rolph

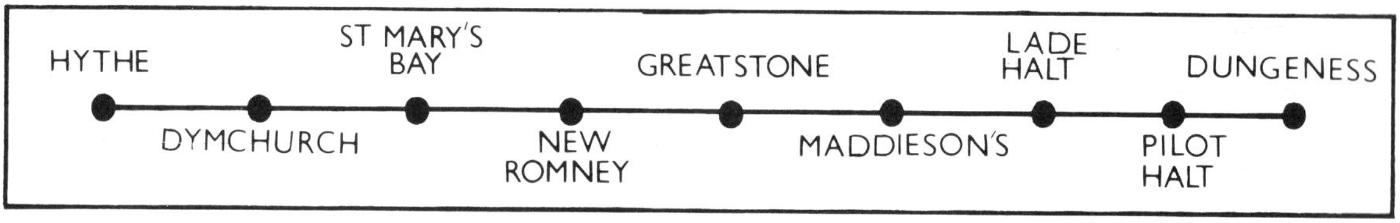

Quainton Railway Society

Location: Adjacent to BR goods only line to Aylesbury. Six miles north of Aylesbury. Turn off A41 at Waddesdon 6 miles NW of Aylesbury, Bucks
Operating society/organisation: Quainton Railway Society Ltd, The Railway Station, Quainton, near Aylesbury, Bucks HP22 4BY
Telephone: St Albans 54904
Car park: Quainton Road — Free parking
Access by public transport: BR Aylesbury station, Red Rover bus. None on Sundays
On site facilities: Souvenir bookshop, light refreshments, steam hauled train rides. Museum of small relics
Public opening: Most weekends. Engines only in steam on advertised open days. 10.00-18.00 on all dates
Special notes: OS Map reference SP738190. A large collection of standard gauge locomotives, together with a most interesting collection of vintage coaching stock much of which was built in the last century

Above: *The nicely restored station at Quainton Road, headquarters of the Quainton Railway Society.* *J. Scrace*

Locomotives

Name	*No*	*Origin*	*Class*	*Type*	*Built*
—	1	Met Rly		4-4-0T	1898
—	0314	LSWR	0298	2-4-0WT	1874
King Edward 1	6024	GWR	'King'	4-6-0	1930
Wightwick Hall	6989	GWR	'Hall'	4-6-0	1948
—	7715	GWR	5700	0-6-0PT	1930
—	9466	GWR	9400	0-6-0PT	1952
—	41298	LMS	2MT	2-6-2T	1951
—	41313	LMS	2MT	2-6-2T	1951
—	46447	LMS	2MT	2-6-0	1950

Industrial locomotives

Name	*No*	*Builder*	*Type*	*Built*
Sydenham	—	A/Porter (3567)	4WTG	1895
Scott	—	Bagnall (2469)	0-4-0ST	1932
Swanscombe	—	Barclay (699)	0-4-0ST	1891
Punch Hull	—	Barclay (776)	0-4-0ST	1896
Alexander	—	Barclay (1865)	0-4-0ST	1926
Tom Parry	—	Barclay (2015)	0-4-0ST	1935
GF3	—	Barclay (1477)	0-4-0F	1916
—	—	Barclay (2243)	0-4-0F	1948
Osram	—	Fowler (20067)	0-4-0DM	1933
—	3	H/Leslie (3717)	0-4-0ST	1928
Sir Thomas	—	H/Clarke (1334)	0-6-0T	1918
Millom	—	H/Clarke (1742)	0-4-0ST	1946
Trym	—	Hunslet (287)	0-4-0ST	1882
Juno	—	Hunslet (3850)	0-6-0ST	1958
—	66	Hunslet (3890)	0-6-0ST	1964
—	—	K/Stuart (K4428)	0-4-0DM	1929
Coventry No 1	—	NBL (24564)	0-6-0ST	1939
Hornpipe	—	Peckett (1756)	0-4-0ST	1928
Jill	—	Peckett (1900)	0-4-0T	1936
—	—	Peckett (2104)	0-4-0ST	1948
—	—	Peckett (2105)	0-4-0ST	1948
James	—	Peckett (2129)	0-4-0ST	1952
Tarmac	—	Hibberd (3765)	0-4-0DM	1955
Isebrook	—	Sentinel (6515)	4wVBTG	1926
—	11	Sentinel (9366)	4wVBTG	1945
—	7	Sentinel (9376)	4wVBTG	1947

Stock
3 ex-BR Mk1 coaches
6 LNWR and 2 LMSR coaches
2 GCR, 2 GNR and 1 LNER coach
A number of box vans, open wagons and miscellaneous vehicles

Owners
6024 (the 6024 Preservation Society Ltd)
41298 (the Ivatt Locomotive Trust)
41313 (the Ivatt Locomotive Trust)
46447 (the Ivatt Locomotive Trust)
6989 (the Quainton Railway (Wightwick Hall) Society Ltd)
9466 (the 9466 Group)

Didcot Railway Centre

Location: Adjacent to BR station, Didcot, Oxfordshire. Access via station subway
Operating society/organisation: Great Western Society Ltd, Didcot Railway Centre, Didcot, Oxon
Car park: Didcot BR station
Access by public transport: Didcot BR station
On site facilities: Refreshments and souvenir sales, rides are available on the demonstration lines
Public opening: Saturdays, Sundays and Bank Holidays April-October. Steaming days first and last Sundays of each month, all August Sundays, Bank Holidays
Special notes: Special steam days for school children 8, 9, 10 July

Above right: ***A selection of restored GWR motive power on display at Didcot Railway Centre.*** *Great Western Society*

Below: ***The Great Western Society's Didcot Railway Centre boasts a turntable among its facilities, here seen playing host to the society's 'Manor' Class 4-6-0 No 7808*** **Cookham Manor.** *Great Western Society*

Locomotives

Name	*No*	*Origin*	*Class*	*Type*	*Built*
Trojan	1340	GWR	Avonside (1380)	0-4-0ST	1897
—	1466	GWR	1400	0-4-2T	1936
—	3650	GWR	5700	0-6-0PT	1939
—	3738	GWR	5700	0-6-0PT	1937
—	3822	GWR	2884	2-8-0	1940
—	4144	GWR	5100	2-6-2T	1946
Maindy Hall	4942	GWR	'Hall'	4-6-0	1929
—	5322	GWR	4300	2-6-0	1917
—	5572	GWR	4575	2-6-2T	1927
Nunney Castle	5029	GWR	'Castle'	4-6-0	1934
Earl Bathurst	5051	GWR	'Castle'	4-6-0	1936
Hinderton Hall	5900	GWR	'Hall'	4-6-0	1931
—	6106	GWR	6100	2-6-2T	1931
—	6697	GWR	5600	0-6-2T	1928
Burton Agnes Hall	6998	GWR	'Hall'	4-6-0	1949
—	7202	GWR	7200	2-8-2T	1934
Cookham Manor	7808	GWR	'Manor'	4-6-0	1938
—	1363	GWR	1361	0-6-0PT	1910
Winston Churchill	34051	SR	BB	4-6-2	1946
—	D7018	BR	35	B-B	1962
Pontyberem	2	Bury Port & Gwendraeth Valley Rly		0-6-0ST	1900
Shannon	5	Wantage Tramway		0-4-0WT	1857

Stock
Over 40 ex-GWR coaches are preserved on the site along with numerous ex-GWR freight wagons

Owners
34051 (on loan from the National Railway Museum)
5 (on loan from the National Railway Museum)
D7018 (Diesel & Electric Group)

Brockham Museum (of Narrow Gauge Railways)

Location: Chalkpit Lane, Betchworth, Surrey RH3 7EZ. Situated in a disused limeworks at the foot of Boxhill, Surrey
Operating society/organisation: Brockham Museum Trust, c/o 14 Sydney Road, Haywards Heath, West Sussex RH16 1PZ
Car park: At the site
Access by public transport: London Country bus route No 414 to Brockham Lane, BR to Betchworth (1 mile) or Dorking (North) (2 miles — or by No 414 bus)
On site facilities: Shop. 2ft gauge demonstration railway with goods and passenger trains
Public opening: Third Sunday of the month, April-September 11.30-17.30
Special notes: Access to the site is via an unmarked track off the A25 between Dorking and Reigate. Turn left 60yds after Brockham Lane coming from Dorking or right 100yds after the 'Arkle Manor' public house from Reigate. Care should be taken when entering as the access is across BR tracks, please wait until the gates are opened for you. Do not park in the lane leading to the museum

Locomotives

Name	*No*	*Builder*	*Type*	*Built*
Polar Bear	—	Bagnall (1781)	2-4-0T	1905
Peter	—	Bagnall (2067)	0-4-0T	1918
*Townsend Hook**	—	F/Jennings (172L)	0-4-0T	1880
Scaldwell	—	Peckett (1316)	0-6-0ST	1913
—	23	Spence	0-4-0T	1921
Monty	6	Orenstein & Koppel (7269)	4wDM	1936
The Major	7	Orenstein & Koppel (7741)	4wDM	1937
—	2	Ransomes & Rapier (80)	4wDM	1937
—	—	Hudson-Hunslet (3097)	4wDM	1944
—	2	R/Hornsby (166024)	4wDM	1933
—	(LR 3041)	M/Rail (Simplex) (1320)	4wDM (ex-PM)	1918
Peldon	—	John Fowler (21295)	4wDM	1936
—	—	Orenstein & Koppel (6193)	4wDM	1937
—	—*	Lister (29890)	4wPM	1946
—	27*	M/Rail (Simplex) (5863)	4wDM	1934
—	(LR 2593)	M/Rail (Simplex) (872)	4wPM	1918
—	WD 904	Wickham (3403)	2w+2PMR	1943
—	2	Wingrove & Rogers (5031)	4wBE	1953

Stock
RAF Fauld bogie coach (1940)
Rye & Camber Tramway bogie coach (incomplete) (1895)
Groudle Glen Railway 4-wheel coach* (1896)
41 other varied pieces of narrow gauge rolling stock plus numerous miscellaneous exhibits including track, signals, etc

*Indicates item that *may not* be on site for all or part of 1980 season

Science Museum

Location: South Kensington
Operating society/organisation: Science Museum, Exhibition Road, South Kensington, London SW7
Telephone: 01-589 3459
Access by public transport: South Kensington underground station
On site facilities: Small book shop and refreshments
Public opening: Weekdays 10.00-18.00, Sundays 14.30-18.00 (admission free)
Special notes: Static exhibits only

Locomotives

Name	*No*	*Origin*	*Class*	*Type*	*Built*
Caerphilly Castle	4073	GWR	'Castle'	4-6-0	1923
Deltic	—	E/Electric	—	Co-Co	1955
Rocket	—	L&MR	—	0-2-2	1829
Sans Pareil	—	L&MR	—	0-4-0	1829
*Novelty**	—	St Helen's Rly	—	0-4-0	1829
	1	C&SLR	—	4wE	1890

Industrial locomotive

Name	*No*	*Builder*	*Type*	*Built*
Bauxite	2	B/Hawthorn (305)	0-4-0ST	1874

Stock

LPTB underground coach, No 3327 (built 1927)
*Replica

London Transport Museum

Location: Covent Garden, London WC2
Operating society/organisation: London Transport Museum
Telephone: Not yet known (via 01-222 1234)
Access by public transport: Underground to Covent Gdn, Leicester Sq or Charing Cross. Buses to Strand or Aldwych
On site facilities: Coffee bar, lecture room
Public opening: Daily 10.00 to 18.00 Closed Christmas Day, Boxing Day
Special Notes: The new museum will open in spring 1980

Locomotives

Name	*No*	*Origin*	*Class*	*Type*	*Built*
	23	Met Rly	A	4-4-0T	1866
John Hampden	5	Met Rly		Bo-Bo	1922

Industrial locomotive

Origin	*Builder*	*Type*	*Built*
Wotton Tramway	A/Porter (807)	0-4-0TG	1872

Electric stock

No 4248 District Rly Q23 motor coach
No 11182 LPTB 1938 stock motor coach
No 400 Met Rly Steam control trailer coach 1899
No 30 City & South London Rly 'Padded Cell' coach 1890

Stock:

1 Met Rly milk van
3 electric trams
3 horse buses
10 motor buses
2 trolley buses

Below: ***Chesham shuttle coach at Ruislip Depot in May 1979, now in the London Transport Museum.*** *London Transport Executive*

Dart Valley Railway (Torbay section)

Headquarters: Paignton Park station, Paignton, Devon
Telephone: Paignton 555872
Main station: Paignton Park
Other public stations: Goodrington, Churston, Kingswear
Car parks: Paignton municipal car park, Dartmouth (ferry to Kingswear)
Access by public transport: Several local buses serve the station which is adjacent to the BR station at Paignton
Refreshment facilities: Kingswear
Souvenir shop: Paignton
Museum: Buckfastleigh (Dart Valley line)
Depot: Buckfastleigh (Dart Valley line)
Passenger trains: Paignton-Kingswear (7 miles) views of Torbay and Dart estuary, 492 yd tunnel
Period of public operation: Easter, Sundays early May, daily from mid-May-September

Locomotives

Name	*No*	*Origin*	*Class*	*Type*	*Built*
—	4588	GWR	4575	2-6-2T	1927
—	5239	GWR	4200	2-8-0T	1924
Lydham Manor	7827	GWR	7800	4-6-0	1950
—	2192	BR	03	0-6-0DM	1961

Industrial locomotive

Name	*No*	*Builder*	*Type*	*Built*
Enterprise	—	H/Clarke (D810)	0-6-0DM	1953

Stock
7 ex-BR Mk1 coaches
3 ER Suburban coaches (ex-Kings Cross)
Stock is sometimes transferred to and from the Dart Valley line

Owner
7827 (the Dart Valley Association)

Below: ***A down train headed by ex-GWR 2-8-0T No 5239 passes 2-6-2T No 4588 on an up train at Churston on the Torbay section of the Dart Valley Railway.*** *M. S. Wilkins*

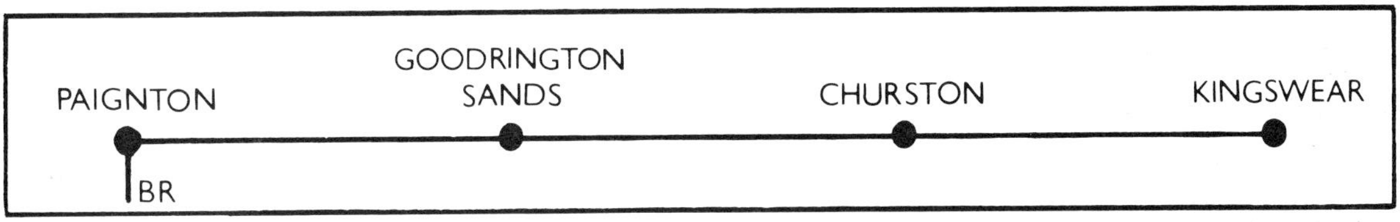

Dart Valley Railway (Buckfastleigh section)

Headquarters: Dart Valley Railway, Buckfastleigh station, Buckfastleigh, Devon
Telephone: Buckfastleigh 2338
Main Station: Buckfastleigh
Other public stations: Staverton Bridge, Totnes (no public access)
Car park: Buckfastleigh
Access by public transport: A38 road between Exeter and Plymouth
Refreshment facilities: Buckfastleigh
Souvenir shop: Buckfastleigh
Museum: Buckfastleigh
Depot: Buckfastleigh
Passenger trains: Buckfastleigh-Totnes (7 miles) alongside the River Dart
Special notes: Sundays April-Mid May and Easter then Sunday to Friday mid May-early September

Locomotives

Name	*No*	*Origin*	*Class*	*Type*	*Built*
—	1420	GWR	1400	0-4-2T	1933
—	1450	GWR	1400	0-4-2T	1935
—	1369	GWR	1366	0-6-0PT	1934
—	1638	GWR	1600	0-6-0PT	1951
—	4555	GWR	4500	2-6-2T	1924
Dumbleton Hall	4920	GWR	'Hall'	4-6-0	1929
—	6430	GWR	6400	0-6-0PT	1937
—	6435	GWR	6400	0-6-0PT	1937
—	80064	BR	4MT	2-6-4T	1954
—	30587	LSWR	0298	2-4-0WT	1874

Industrial locomotives

Name	*No*	*Builder*	*Type*	*Built*
—	1	Peckett (2031)	0-4-0ST	1942
—	1690	Peckett (1690)	0-4-0ST	1926
—	—	Bagnall (2766)	0-6-0ST	1944

Stock
4 ex-BR Mk1 coaches
12 ex-GWR coaches
1 LNER buffet coach
1 Pullman observation coach
1 steam cranes
1 LNER buffet coach

Owners
4920 (the Dumbleton Hall Preservation Society)
30587 (on loan from the National Railway Museum)
80064 (the 80064 Locomotive Group)

Left: ***GWR 0-6-0PT No 1638 on a Buckfastleigh-Totnes train near Buckfastleigh.*** *L. A. Nixon*

West Somerset Railway

Headquarters: West Somerset Railway, The Railway Station, Minehead, Somerset
Telephone: Minehead 4996
Main station: Minehead
Other public stations: Dunster, Blue Anchor, Washford, Watchet, Williton, Stogumber, Crowcombe, Bishop's Lydeard
Car parks: Minehead, Williton. Some parking at all stations
Access by public transport: Nearest BR station, Taunton with connecting bus service as timetable
Refreshment facilities: Minehead
Souvenir shops: Minehead, Bishop's Lydeard (limited opening)
Museum: Somerset & Dorset Railway Museum Trust, Washford
Depots: Bishop's Lydeard, Washford, Williton, Minehead
Passenger trains: Diesel trains to Williton (10 miles) and Bishop's Lydeard (20 miles). Steam trains to Blue Anchor (3½ miles), Williton and Bishop's Lydeard
Period of public operation: Diesel trains to Williton (Mondays to Fridays) and to Bishop's Lydeard (Saturdays) with connecting coach to Taunton and BR throughout the year. Steam trains operate April-October

Locomotives

Name	*No*	*Origin*	*Class*	*Type*	*Built*
—	78	LBSCR	A1X	0-6-0T	1880
—	88	S&DJR	7F	2-8-0	1925
—	4561	GWR	4500	2-6-2T	1924
—	5521	GWR	4575	2-6-2T	1927
—	5542	GWR	4575	2-6-2T	1928
—	6412	GWR	6400	0-6-0PT	1934
—	D7017	BR	35	B-B	1962
—	D2994	BR	07	0-6-0DE	1962

Industrial locomotives

Name	*No*	*Builder*	*Type*	*Built*
Portbury	S3	Avonside (1764)	0-6-0ST	1917
Vulcan	—	Bagnall (2994)	0-6-0ST	1950
Victor	—	Bagnall (2996)	0-6-0ST	1951
—	—	Bagnall (2473)	0-4-0ST	1932
Whitehead	1163	Peckett (1163)	0-4-0ST	1908
Isabel	—	H/Leslie (3437)	0-6-0ST	1919
Kilmersdon	—	Peckett (1788)	0-4-0ST	1929

Below: ***A two-car diesel unit forms the 10.35 from Minehead on the West Somerset Railway, here seen arriving at Bishops Lydeard, from where there is a bus connection to Taunton.*** *S. J. Edge*

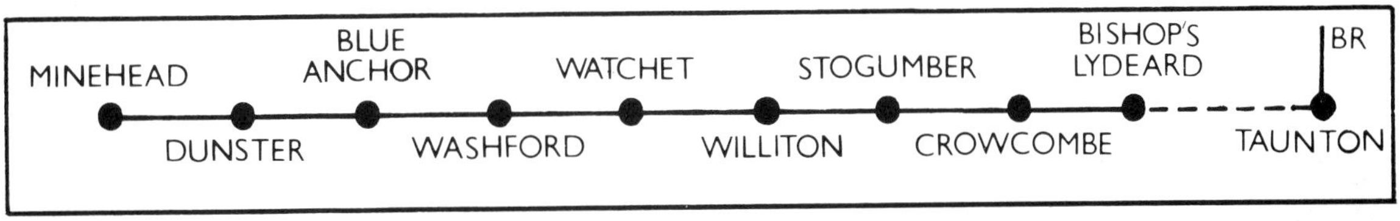

Stock
6 ex-BR Mk1 coaches
2 ex-BR suburban coaches
4 ex-GWR camping coaches
5 ex-BR Pullman cars
1 ex-LNER coach
1 ex-SR 'Ironclad' coach
2 Park Royal 2-car diesel units
1 ex-GWR Hawksworth coach
More than 20 freight vehicles

Owners
S3 (the Somerset & Dorset Museum Trust)
Isabel (the Somerset & Dorset Museum Trust)
Kilmersdon (the Somerset & Dorset Museum Trust)
88 (the Somerset & Dorset Museum Trust)
Bagnall 2473 (the Somerset & Dorset Museum Trust)
D7017 (the Diesel and Electric Group)

East Somerset Railway

Headquarters: East Somerset Railway, Cranmore Railway Co Ltd, Cranmore, Somerset
Telephone: Cranmore 417
Main station: Cranmore
Car park: Cranmore
Refreshment facilities: Cranmore
Souvenir shop: Cranmore
Depot: Cranmore
Passenger trains: Line extension to Merryfield Lane open in 1980, subject to Light Railway Order
Special notes: Open Sundays in January and February and New Year Bank Holiday only. Open daily for rest of year with an engine in steam on Sundays and Bank Holidays from mid-March to mid-October

Locomotives

Name	*No*	*Origin*	*Class*	*Type*	*Built*
Stowe	928	SR	'Schools'	4-4-0	1934
—	32110	LBSCR	E1	0-6-0T	1877
—	47493	LMS	3F	0-6-0T	1927
The Green Knight	75029	BR	4MT	4-6-0	1954
Black Prince	92203	BR	9F	2-10-0	1959

Industrial locomotives

Name	*No*	*Builder*	*Type*	*Built*
Lord Fisher	—	Barclay (1398)	0-4-0ST	1915
Glenfield	—	Barclay (1791)	0-4-0ST	1920
—	—	Dubs (4101)	0-4-0CT	1901
—	68005	RSH (7169)	0-6-0ST	1944

Stock
5 ex-BR Mk1 coaches
1 ex-LMS coach
Small number of wagons

Owners
Lord Fisher (the Lord Fisher Locomotive Group)
Glenfield (the Lord Fisher Locomotive Group)
47493 (the Lord Fisher Locomotive Group)
68005 (the Lord Fisher Locomotive Group)
Dubs 4101 (the Lord Fisher Locomotive Group)

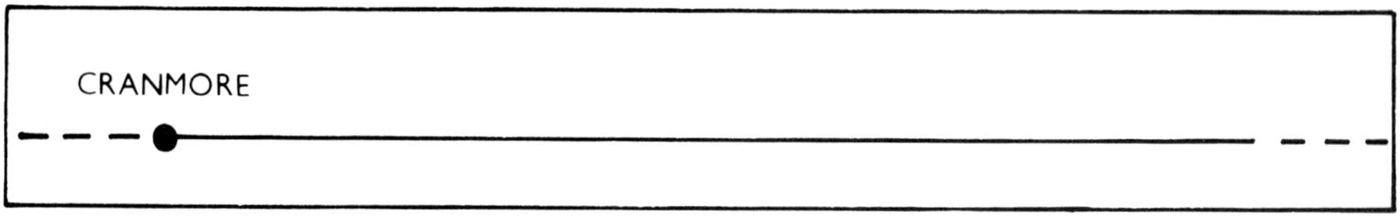

Below: ***'Jinty' 0-6-0T No 47493 in operation on the East Somerset Railway, outside the replica GWR engine shed at Cranmore.***
John Titlow

Ex-SE&CR 'C' 0-6-0 No 592 in action on the Bluebell Railway. *J. H. Cooper-Smith*

Bristol Suburban Railway

Location: Bitton station
Operating society/organisation: Bristol Surburban Railway Society, Bitton station, Bristol, Avon
Car park: Bitton
Access by public transport: Bristol Omnibus service No 332 Bath-Bristol
On site facilities: Toilets, snack bar
Public opening: Every weekend, steam days for 1980. 8/9 March, 4-7 April, 3-5 May, 29 June-6 July (schools' week) 20-21 September, 4-5 October, 13/14 20/21 26-8 December

Locomotive

Name	*No*	*Origin*	*Class*	*Type*	*Built*
—	45379	LMS	5MT	4-6-0	1937

Industrial locomotives

Name	*No*	*Builder*	*Type*	*Built*
Edwin Hulse	2	Avonside (1798)	0-6-0ST	1918
—	3	F/Walker (242)	0-6-0ST	1874
Fonmon	—	Peckett (1936)	0-6-0ST	1924

Stock
1 ex-BR Mk1 coach
3 open wagons
2 ex-LMS box vans
1 LMS refrigerated box van
1 LNER refrigated box van
1 GWR refrigerated box van

Dowty Railway Preservation Society

Location: Northway Lane, Ashchurch
Operating society/organisation: Dowty Railway Preservation Society c/o Dowty Sports & Social Society Ashchurch, near Tewkesbury, Glos
Car park: Within the site
On site facilities: A souvenir shop.
Public opening: Every Sunday afternoon, with engines in steam on certain dates
Special notes: It is expected that the society will have to change to a nearby site during 1980

Industrial standard gauge locomotives

Name	*No*	*Builder*	*Type*	*Built*
Cadbury	1	Avonside (1977)	0-4-0T	1925
Drake	—	Barclay (2086)	0-4-0ST	1940
—	—	Barclay (2126)	0-4-0F	1942
—	2	Barclay (2221)	0-4-0ST	1946

Stock
2 ex-GWR coaches
5 goods wagons

Industrial narrow gauge locomotives

Name	*No*	*Builder*	*Type*	*Built*
George B	—	Hunslet (680)	0-4-0ST	1898
Justine	—	Jung (939)	0-4-0WT	1906
—	2	Lister (34523)	4wDM	—
—	3	M/Rail (4565)	4wPM	1928
Spitfire	—	M/Rail (7053)	4wPM	1937
—	1	R/Hornsby (166010)	4wDM	1932
—	L5	R/Hornsby (18120)	4wDM	1936
—	802	R/Hornsby (221645)	4wDM	1944
—	—	R/Hornsby (354028)	4wDM	1953

Stock
1 coach
14 wagons

Norchard Steam Centre

Location: Adjacent to the BR line from Lydney to Parkend, on the B4234, $\frac{1}{2}$ mile off A48 at Lydney
Operating society/organisation: Dean Forest Railway Society Ltd, Norchard Steam Centre, New Mills, Lydney, Forest of Dean, Glos
Telephone: Dean (0594) 43423

Locomotives

Name	*No*	*Origin*	*Class*	*Type*	*Built*
—	5541	GWR	4575	2-6-2T	1928
—	9681	GWR	5700	0-6-0PT	1949

Car park: (Adequate for cars and coaches — no charge)
Access by public transport: B4234 from Lydney. National Welsh bus service No 40 passes the site
On site facilities: A shop and refreshments are available at Norchard along with a small museum
Public opening: Every Saturday and Sunday 11.00-17.00 Steam days are normally every Bank Holiday Sunday and Monday and every Sunday in August
Special notes: For 1980 it is expected that steam train rides on Steam Days will be over the $\frac{1}{3}$ mile track to Middle Forge from the station at Norchard

The Society aims to acquire and operate the Lydney-Parkend branch line as and when put up for disposal by BR

Industrial locomotives

Name	*No*	*Builder*	*Type*	*Built*
—	3806	Hunslet (3806)	0-6-0ST	1953
—	—	Hunslet (2145)	0-4-0DM	1940
Uskmouth No 1	—	Peckett (2147)	0-4-0ST	1952

Stock
4 ex-GWR coaches
2 Wickham trolleys
1 steam crane Thos Smith (Rodley) No TS 5027
17+ wagons

Owners
9681 (the Forest Pannier Tank Fund)
5541 (the Forest Prairie Fund)

Below: *Peckett 0-4-0ST* Uskmouth 1 *hauls ex-GWR auto-trailer No 167 at Norchard Steam Centre during a 1979 open day.* *P. Skinner*

Swanage Railway Centre

Location: Swanage station
Operating society/organisation: Swanage Railway Co Ltd, Station Master's House, Railway Station, Swanage, Dorset
Car park: Swanage
Access by public transport: Hants & Dorset buses from Bournemouth, Poole and Wareham stop outside station
On site facilities: Shop and light refreshments
Public opening: Every Saturday & Sunday and Public Holidays except Christmas Day

Locomotives

Name	*No*	*Origin*	*Class*	*Type*	*Built*
—	6695	GWR	5600	0-6-2T	1928
—	80078	BR	4MT	2-6-4T	1954

Industrial locomotive

Name	*No*	*Builder*	*Type*	*Built*
—	—	Planet (2054)	4wPM	1938

Above: ***Festiniog Railway 2-4-0ST* Blanche *passes* Boston Lodge *works' entrance in 1975.*** *R. Russell*

Below: ***'Manor' 4-6-0 No 7819* Hinton Manor *runs round its train at* Bewdley *on the* Severn Valley Railway *on 5 March 1978.*** *W. A. Sharman*

7819

Above: ***Members of the Southern Steam Trust engaged in the work of extending their track past the locomotive shed at Swanage.*** *Southern Steam Trust*

Stock
Bulleid coach
LSWR coach body
2 ex-SR vans

Owners
6695 (the Great Western Railway Preservation Group)
80078 (the Southern Steam Trust)

Swindon GWR Museum

Location: Faringdon Road, Swindon, Wiltshire
Operating society/organisation: Borough of Thamesdown, GWR Museum, Faringdon Road, Swindon, Wiltshire
Telephone: Swindon 26161 ext 562
Car park: Swindon BR station and street parking
Access by public transport: Swindon BR (10minutes)
On site facilities: A selection of souvenirs is available
Public opening: Weekdays 10.00-17.00, Sundays 14.00-17.00. Closed Good Friday, Christmas Day, Boxing Day and New Year Day
Special Notes: The Museum also houses a considerable number of photographs depicting scenes of the GWR

Locomotives

Name	*No*	*Origin*	*Class*	*Type*	*Built*
—	2516	GWR	2301	0-6-0	1887
City of Truro	3717	GWR	'City'	4-4-0	1903
Lode Star	4003	GWR	'Star'	4-6-0	1907
—	9400	GWR	9400	0-6-0PT	1947
*North Star**	—	GWR	—	2-2-2	1837

*Broad gauge replica

Diesel Traction Group

Location: BREL Swindon Works
Operating society/organisation: Diesel Traction Group, 31 Courts Road, Reading, Berks
Public opening: On special works open days only
Special notes: These locomotives are stored on BREL property and are therefore not available for public viewing, they can however be seen from passing trains

Locomotives

Name	*No*	*Origin*	*Class*	*Type*	*Built*
Greyhound	D821	BR	42	B-B	1960
—	D7029	BR	35	B-B	1962

WALES

Gwili Railway

Headquarters: Gwili Railway Company Limited, Bronwydd Arms station, Bronwydd Arms, Carmarthen, Dyfed
Telephone: Neath 2191
Main station: Bronwydd Arms
Other public stations: Cwmdwyfran, Llwyfan Cerrig (to be opened)
Car park: Bronwydd Arms
Access by public transport: Carmarthen BR station, then Crossville bus service No S44. A484 road.
Refreshment facilities: Bronwydd Arms, Llwyfan Cerrig (picnic site)
Souvenir shop: Bronwydd Arms
Depot: Some stock at 'Ironrails', Carmarthen
Passenger trains: $2\frac{1}{2}$-mile return journey
Period of public operation: Weekends July-September, also Bank Holidays, first week of August
Special Notes: Special Enthusiasts weekend last weekend in September. Line being extended northwards

Locomotives

Name	*No*	*Origin*	*Class*	*Type*	*Built*
Dinmore Manor	7820	GWR	'Manor'	4-6-0	1950

Industrial locomotives

Name	*No*	*Builder*	*Type*	*Built*
Merlin/Myrddin	—	Peckett (1967)	0-4-0ST	1939
—	1903	Peckett (1903)	0-4-0ST	1936
—	—	R/Hornsby (207103)	4wDM	1941
—	7058	RSH (7058)	0-4-0ST	1942

Stock
1 ex-BR diesel unit trailer car
1 ex-BR Mk1 coach
Various vans and open wagons

Llangollen Railway Society

Location: Llangollen station, A542 from Ruabon, A5 from Shrewsbury, A5 from Betws y Coed
Operating society/organisation: Llangollen Railway Society Ltd, Llangollen station, Llangollen, Clwyd
Telephone: Llangollen 860951
Car park: Llangollen
Access by public transport: Nearest station: Ruabon (2hr service), then Crosville bus service No D1 to Llangollen or Nos D93/D94
On site facilities: Shop and refreshments are available. GPO public telephone. 'Bridge' Taxi service operates out of forecourt. (phone 860567)
Public opening: Weekends throughout the year, daily during the tourist season. Several steam days are held during the year, most bank holidays and during International Eisteddfod week in July
Special notes: The railway hope to commence public operations during the year subject to granting of light railway order

Above: ***Llangollen station, beside the river Dee is returning to life again under the auspices of the Llangollen Railway Society.*** *Joma Enterprises*

On the Ravenglass & Eskdale Railway, 2-6-2 Northern Rock at Irton Road in 1976.
K. Ellwood

Industrial locomotives

Name	*No*	*Builder*	*Type*	*Built*
Eliseg	—	Fowler (22753)	0-4-0DM	1939
—	—	Fowler (400007)	0-4-0DM	1947
Richboro	—	H/Clarke (1243)	0-6-0T	1917
—	1243	Hunslet (1243)	0-6-0T	1917
Austin No1	—	Kitson (5439)	0-6-0ST	1932
—	14	H/Clarke (D1012)	0-4-0DM	1956
—	—	Sentinel (9596)	4wVBTG	1955

Stock

3 coaches
4 wagons
1 GWR steam crane (working)
1 GWR siphon G
1 GWR brake van
1 SR 'BY' parcels van

Bala Lake Railway (Rheilffordd Llyn Tegid)

Headquarters: Rheilffordd Llyn Tegid (Bala Lake Railway) Llanuwchllyn, Bala, Gwynedd
Telephone: Llanuwchllyn 666/Bala 520226
Main station: Llanuwchllyn
Other public stations: Llangower, Bala
Car parks: Llanuwchllyn, Llangower
Access by public transport: Crosville bus services Nos D93 and D94 to both Bala and Llanuwchllyn (from Wrexham to Barmouth)
Refreshment facilities: Llanuwchllyn. Large picnic site with toilet facilities by lake at Llangower
Souvenir shop: Llanuwchllyn
Museum: Large collection of antique railway equipment, mostly in daily use
Depot: Llanuwchllyn
Passenger trains: 1ft 11$\frac{1}{2}$in gauge line Llanuwchllyn — Bala (4$\frac{1}{2}$miles). Journey takes 27 minutes in each direction
Period of public operation: Daily Easter until September then weekends until mid-October
Special notes: Special parties and chartered trains by arrangement during July and August. At other times just turn up

Industrial Locomotives

Name	*No*	*Builder*	*Type*	*Built*
Holy War	—	Hunslet (779)	0-4-0ST	1902
Maid Marian	—	Hunslet (822)	0-4-0ST	1903
Meirionnydd	—	Severn Lamb (7322)	Bo-Bo	1973
Alice	—	Hunslet (780)	0-4-0ST	1902
—	—	R/Hornsby (194771)	4wDM	1939
—	—	R/Hornsby (200744)	4wDM	1940
—	—	Lister (44052)	4wDM	1958
—	—	Hudson (38384)	4wDM	1930
—	—	Motorail (5821)	4wDM	1934
—	—	R/Hornsby (209430)	4wDM	1942
—	—	R/Hornsby (189972)	4wDM	1938
—	—	Hibberd (FH2544)	4wDM	1941
—	—	Hunslet (758248)	4wDM	1940

Owner
Maid Marian (the Maid Marian Locomotive Fund)

Right: ***Hunslet 0-4-0ST* Maid Marian *of the Bala Lake Railway poses in front of the ex-GWR signalbox at Llanuwchllyn.***
B. Morrison

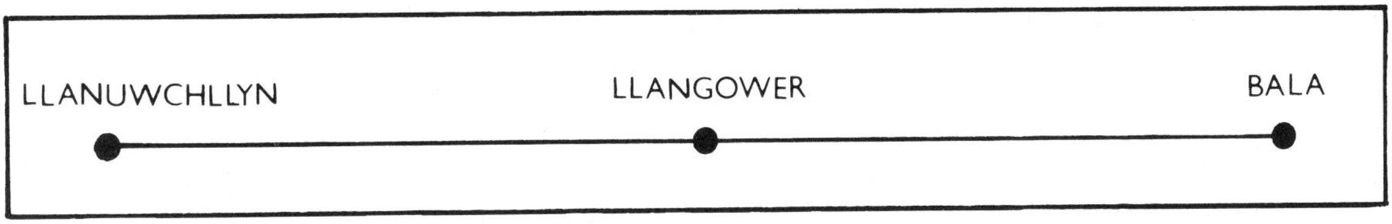

Fairbourne Railway

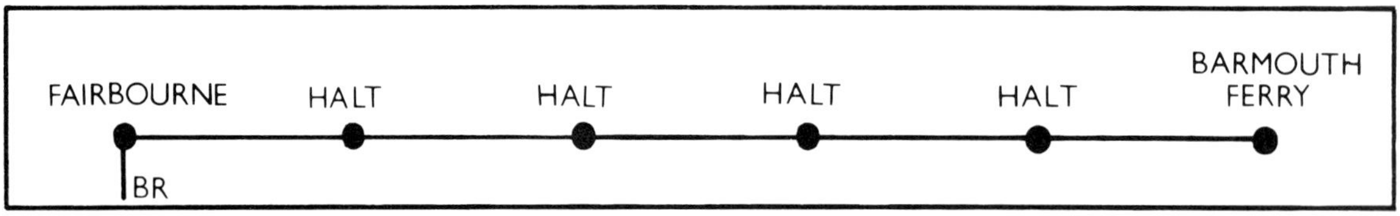

Headquarters: Fairbourne Railway Ltd, Beach Road, Fairbourne, Gwynedd, LL38 2EX
Telephone: 0341-250362
Main station: Fairbourne
Other public stations: Barmouth Ferry, Public halts at Bathing Beach, Golf House, Passing Loop and Penrhyn Bridge
Car parks: Fairbourne and adjacent to Bathing Beach & Golf House halts
Access by public transport: Fairbourne BR station. Crosville bus service No S28 Dolgellau-Towyn A493 road
Refreshment facilities: Fairbourne and Ferry — with picnic site
Souvenir shop: Fairbourne
Depot: Fairbourne
Passenger trains: 15in gauge line Fairbourne-Barmouth Ferry (just under 2 miles). Journey time approx 20 minutes each way. Trains connect with Barmouth Ferry
Period of public operation: Easter to mid-October subject to timetable change for 1980

Locomotives

Name	*No*	*Builder*	*Type*	*Built*
Count Louis	—	B/Lowke (32)	4-4-2	1924
Ernest W. Twining	—	G&S (10)	4-6-2	1949
Katie	—	G&S (14)	2-4-2	1954
Sian	—	Guest (18)	2-4-2	1963
Rachel	—	G&S (15)	0-6-0DM	1959
Sylvia	—	G&S (14A)	Bo-BoPH	1961
Gwril	—	Lister (20886)	4wPM	1941

Stock
17 coaches
1 canteen coach
8 wagons (including 2 bogie tipper wagons)

Special notes: A flag is flown at Barmouth Ferry when trains are running. During inclement weather the service may be restricted or cancelled. Extra trains and special parties by arrangement with the manager.

Llanberis Lake Railway (Rheilfford Llyn Llanberis)

Headquarters: Llanberis Lake Railway, Gilfach Ddu, Llanberis, Gwynedd
Telephone: Llanberis 549
Main station: Llanberis (Padarn Park/ Gilfachddu)
Other public stations: Penllyn, Cei Llydan
Car park: Llanberis (Padarn Country Park)
Refreshment facilities: Padarn Park
Souvenir shop: Padarn Park
Passenger trains: 1ft $11\frac{1}{2}$in gauge line Llanberis-Penllyn-Llanberis (4 miles)
Period of public operation: Daily April-September

Industrial locomotives

Name	*No*	*Builder*	*Type*	*Built*
Elidir	1	Hunslet (493)	0-4-0ST	1889
Wild Aster	2	Hunslet (849)	0-4-0ST	1904
Dolbadarn	3	Hunslet (1430)	0-4-0ST	1922
Helen Kathryn	5	Henschel (28035)	0-4-0T	1948
Ginette Marie	6	Jung (7509)	0-4-0WT	1937
Twll Coed	8	R/Hornsby (268878)	4wDM	1952
Dolgarrog	9	M/Rail (22154)	4wDM	1962
Yr Enfys	10	R/Hornsby (297030)	4wDM	1952
Cernyw	11	R/Hornsby (200748)	4wDM	1940
Mor Leidr	12	R/Hornsby (375316)	4wDM	1954
Rhydychen	14	M/Rail (11177)	4wDM	1966
Garret	17	M/Rail (7902)	4wDM	1939
Llanelli	18	R/Hornsby (451901)	4wDM	1961
—	—	R/Hornsby (441427)	4wDM	1961

Stock
12 bogie coaches
20 wagons

Welsh Highland Railway

Location: Porthmadog, adjacent to BR station
Operating society/organisation: Welsh Highland Light Railway (1964) Ltd, Gelerts Farm, Madoc Street West, Porthmadog, Gwynedd
Telephone: Porthmadog 3402 (weekends and summer Bank holidays only)
Car park: Porthmadog BR station
Access by public transport: Rail service to Porthmadog BR station. Crosville bus to Porthmadog
On site facilities: Sales shop at car park
Public opening: Train service subject to DOT inspection
Special notes: Proposed service at weekends from Whitsun-September and daily during August

Industrial locomotives

Name	*No*	*Builder*	*Type*	*Built*
Gertrude	—	Barclay (1578)	0-6-0T	1918
Russell	—	Hunslet (901)	2-6-2T	1906
Pedemoura	—	O&K (10808)	0-6-0WT	1924
Karen	—	Peckett (2024)	0-4-2T	1942
Cilgwyn	—	R/Hornsby (175414)	4wDM	1936
Kinnerley	—	R/Hornsby (297030)	4wDM	1952
—	—	R/Hornsby (327904)	4wDM	1951

Stock
A collection of rolling stock including a bogie coach and numerous service vehicles.

Snowdon Mountain Railway

Headquarters: Snowdon Mountain Railway Ltd, Llanberis, Gwynedd LL55-47Y
Telephone: Llanberis 223
Main station: Llanberis
Other public stations: Summit
Car park: Llanberis
Access by public transport: Bangor BR station then by bus No 76 Caernarfon to Llanberis by Crosville bus service Nos 94-98
Refreshment facilities: Llanberis, Summit
Souvenir shops: Llanberis, Summit
Depot: Llanberis
Passenger trains: 2ft $7\frac{1}{2}$in gauge line Llanberis-Summit ($4\frac{3}{4}$ miles). Journey time 60 minutes. Departures from Llanberis at 30 minute intervals during peak periods.
Period of public operation: Daily Easter until early October
Special notes: The only British steam rack railway. Return trains will not leave Summit with less than 25 passengers. All trains are subject to weather and traffic restrictions. Special parties by arrangement only

Locomotives

Name	*No*	*Builder*	*Type*	*Built*
Enid	2	SLM (924)	0-4-2T	1895
Wyddfa	3	SLM (925)	0-4-2T	1895
Snowdon	4	SLM (988)	0-4-2T	1896
Moel Siabod	5	SLM (989)	0-4-2T	1896
Padarn	6	SLM (2838)	0-4-2T	1922
Ralph Sadler	7	SLM (2869)	0-4-2T	1923
Eryri	8	SLM (2870)	0-4-2T	1923

All the above were built by Swiss Locomotive Works, Winterthur

Stock
9 semi-open bogie coaches
1 bogie works car
1 4-wheel open wagon

Right: ***On the Snowdon Mountain Railway No 7 waits at Hebron for a descending train to pass.*** *B. Morrison*

Talyllyn Railway

Headquarters: Talyllyn Railway Co, Wharf station, Tywyn, Gwynedd LL36 9EY
Telephone: Tywyn 710472
Main station: Tywyn Wharf
Other public stations: Tywyn Pendre, Rhydyronen, Brynglas, Dolgoch Falls, Abergynolwyn, Nant Gwernol
Car parks: Tywyn Wharf, Dolgoch, Abergynolwyn
Access by public transport: Tywyn BR station. Crosville bus services to Tywyn.
Refreshment facilities: Tywyn Wharf, Dolgoch, Abergynolwyn
Souvenir shops: Tywyn Wharf, Abergynolwyn.
Museum: Tywyn Wharf
Depot: Tywyn Pendre
Passenger trains: 2ft 3in gauge line Tywyn-Nant Gwernol. (7$\frac{1}{2}$ miles)
Period of public operation: Daily early April to end of September. Limited (not daily) in October
Special notes: Family Return tickets are available. Special parties and private charter trains by arrangement. Children under 3 years of age free

Locomotives

Name	*No*	*Builder*	*Type*	*Built*
Talyllyn	1	F/Jennings (42)	0-4-2ST	1865
Dolgoch	2	F/Jennings (63)	0-4-0WT	1866
Sir Haydn	3	Hughes (323)	0-4-2ST	1878
Edward Thomas	4	K/Stuart (4047)	0-4-2ST	1921
Midlander	5	R/Hornsby (200792)	4wDM	1940
Douglas	6	Barclay (1431)	0-4-0WT	1918
Irish Pete	7	Barclay (2263)	0-4-2T	1949
Merseysider	8	R/Hornsby (476108)	4wDH	1964
Alf	6	Hunslet (4136)	0-4-0DM	1950

Stock
13 4-wheel coaches/vans
10 bogie coaches
44 wagons

Narrow Gauge Museum, Tywyn

Name	*No*	*Builder*	*Type*	*Built*
*Katie**	—	Heywood	0-4-0T	1865
Dot	—	B/Peacock (2817)	0-4-0ST	1887
Pet	—	LNWR	0-4-0ST	1865
Rough Pup	—	Hunslet (541)	0-4-0ST	1891
—	2	K/Stuart (721)	0-4-0WT	1902
Jubilee 1867	—	M/Wardle (1382)	0-4-0ST	1897
George Henry	—	de Winton	0-4-0T	1877
—	13	Spence	0-4-0T	1895
Nutty	—	Sentinel	0-4-0VB	1929

*parts only not on public display.

Stock
Various wagons and miscellaneous equipment

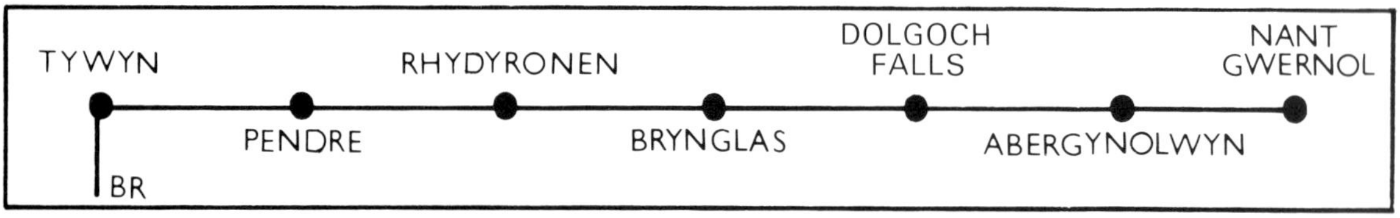

Below: ***No 3* Sir Haydn *heads away from Dolgoch station with a Tywyn-Nant Gwernol train.*** B. Morrison

Vale of Rheidol Railway

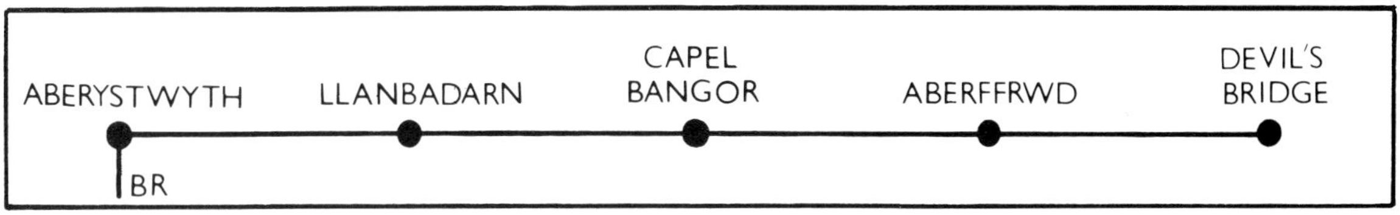

Headquarters: Vale of Rheidol Railway, Aberystwyth, Dyfed
Telephone: Aberystwyth 612377
Main station: Aberystwyth
Other public stations: Devil's Bridge, Rhiwfron, Rheidol Falls, Aberffrwd, Nantyronen, Capel Bangor, Glanrafon, Llanbadarn.
Car parks: Aberystwyth, Devil's Bridge
Access by public transport: Aberystwyth BR station: and Crosville bus services to Aberystwyth
Refreshment facilities: Aberystwyth, Devil's Bridge
Souvenir shop: Devil's Bridge
Depot: Aberystwyth (not open to the public)
Passenger trains: 1ft $11\frac{1}{2}$in gauge line Aberystwyth-Devil's Bridge ($11\frac{1}{2}$ miles)
Period of public operation: Daily Easter-early October
Special notes: Operated by British Rail

Locomotives

Name	*No*	*Origin*	*Type*	*Built*
Owain Glyndwr	7	GWR	2-6-2T	1923
Llywelyn	8	GWR	2-6-2T	1923
Prince of Wales	9	D/Metcalfe	2-6-2T	1902

Stock
16 bogie coaches including 7 second-class closed coaches
1 4-wheel baggage van
12 wagons for maintenance use
1 inspection trolley

Above: ***Springtime sunshine highlights No 8*** **Llywelyn** ***approaching Devils Bridge on the 10.15 from Aberystwyth on 29 May 1979.*** *M. J. Collins*

Welshpool and Llanfair Railway

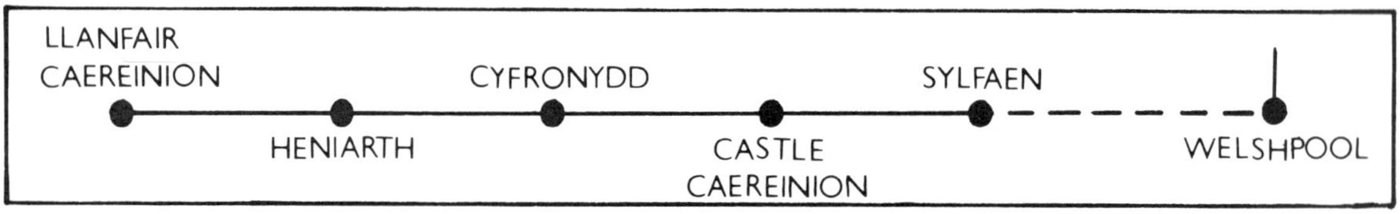

Headquarters: Welshpool & Llanfair Light Railway Preservation Co Ltd, Llanfair Caereinion station, Powys
Telephone: Llanfair Caereinion 441
Main station: Llanfair Caereinion
Other public stations: Castle Caereinion, Sylfaen
Car park: Llanfair Caereinion
Souvenir shops: Llanfair Caereinion
Depot: Llanfair Caereinion
Passenger trains: 2ft 6in gauge line Llanfair Caereinion-Sylfaen ($5\frac{1}{2}$ miles)
Period of public operation: Easter week and weekends to June. Daily June to September, weekends to early October.
Special notes: The railway is extending its line back into Welshpool

Above: ***Bagnall 0-4-4-0T No 6 Monarch of the Welshpool and Llanfair Railway approaches Castle Caereinion on the 17.05 from Sylfaen.***
B. Morrison

Locomotives

Name	*No*	*Builder*	*Type*	*Built*
The Earl	1	B/Peacock (3496)	0-6-0T	1903
The Countess	2	B/Peacock (3497)	0-6-0T	1903
Monarch	6	Bagnall (3024)	0-4-4-0	1953
Chattenden	7	Drewry (2263)	4wDM	1949
Dougal	8	Barclay (2207)	0-4-0T	1946
Sir Drefaldwyn	10	Franco-Belge (2855)	0-8-0T	1944
Raven	11	Hunslet (2251)	4wDM	1940
Joan	12	K/Stuart (4404)	0-6-2T	1927
—	85	Hunslet	2-6-2T	1954
—	—	R/Hornsby (191680)	4wDM	1938

Stock
1 Wickham trolley
7 W&LR wagons
5 ex-Zillertalbahn coaches
4 ex-Sierra Leone coaches

Festiniog Railway

Headquarters: Festiniog Railway Co, Harbour station, Porthmadog, Gwynedd
Telephone: Porthmadog 2384
Main station: Porthmadog Harbour
Other public stations: Minffordd, Penrhyn, Tan-y-Bwlch, Tanygrisiau
Car parks: Porthmadog, Tan-y-Bwlch, Tanygrisiau
Access by public transport: Minffordd BR station. Porthmadog and Tanygrisiau served by local buses
Refreshment facilities: Restaurant at Porthmadog, buffets at Tan-y-Bwlch and Tanygrisiau, also on all trains
Souvenir shops: Porthmadog, Tan-y-Bwlch, Tanygrisiau.
Museum: Porthmadog
Depot: Boston Lodge
Passenger trains: 1ft $11\frac{1}{2}$in gauge line Porthmadog-Tanygrisiau ($24\frac{1}{2}$ mile return journey)
Period of public operation: Weekends February-March. Daily April-October
Special notes: Reduced rates available for early or late return trains, advanced booking essential. Family tickets available

Locomotives

Name	*No*	*Builder*	*Type*	*Built*
Princess	1	G/England	0-4-0ST	1863
Prince	2	G/England	0-4-0ST	1863
Welsh Pony	—	G/England	0-4-0ST	1867
Earl of Merioneth	—	FR	0-4-4-0T	1979
Merddin Emrys	10	FR	0-4-4-0T	1879
Moelwyn	—	Baldwin (49604)	2-4-0DM	1918
Blanche	—	Hunslet (589)	2-4-0ST	1893
Linda	—	Hunslet (590)	2-4-0ST	1893
Britomart	—	Hunslet (707)	0-4-0ST	1899
Mountaineer	—	Alco (57156)	2-6-2T	1916
Livingston Thompson	—	FR	0-4-4-0T	1886
—	—	Peckett (2050)	0-6-0ST	1944
—	—	B/Peacock	0-4-0+0-4-0	1909
Upnor Castle	—	Hibberd (3687)	0-4-0DM	1954
Moel Hebog	—	Hunslet (4113)	0-4-0DM	—
Mary Ann	—	M/Rail	0-4-0DM	1917

7 other 4wDM units

Stock
24 bogie coaches
3 4-wheel coaches
2 brake vans, plus numerous service vehicles.

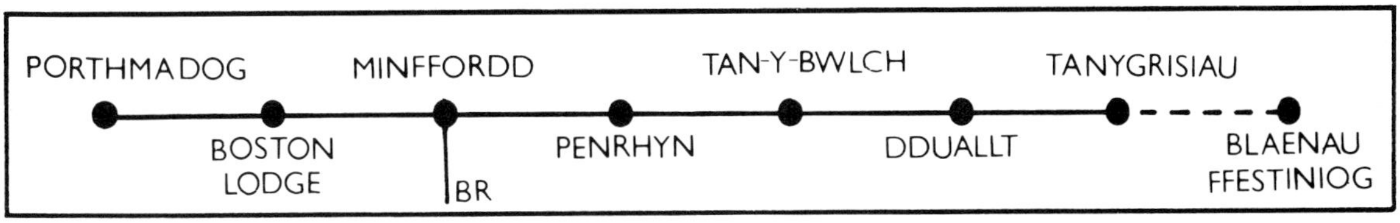

Below: ***The Festiniog Railway's new double-Fairlie*** **Earl of Merioneth** ***approaches Dduallt with the 14.30 from Porthmadog on 27 July 1979.*** *J. Scrace*

Cambrian Railways Society

Location: Oswestry station, Oswald Road, Oswestry, Salop
Operating society/organisation: Cambrian Railways Society Ltd, W. H. Jones, Room 5, Memorial Hall, Smithfield Street, Oswestry, Salop
Car park: Station Road
Public opening: On special open days only

Locomotive

Name	No	Origin	Class	Type	Built
Foxcote Manor	7822	GWR	'Manor'	4-6-0	1950

Industrial locomotives

Name	No	Builder	Type	Built
—	1872	B/Peacock (1827)	0-4-0ST	1879
—	1	H/Clarke	0-4-0DM	1954
Adam	1	Peckett (1430)	0-4-0ST	1916
—	3	Hunslet (D843)	0-6-0DM	1954
—	6	Peckett (2131)	0-4-0ST	1951
—	8	A/Barclay (885)	0-6-0ST	1900
—	322	Planet (3541)	4wDM	1952

Stock
1 GWR auto-trailer
2 tank wagons

Penrhyn Castle Industrial Railway Museum

Location: Llandegai, near Bangor. One mile east of Bangor on the A5
Operating society/organisation: National Trust, Penrhyn Castle, Industrial Railway Museum, Llandegai, near Bangor, Gwynedd
Telephone: Bangor 53084
Car park: Within castle grounds
Access by public transport: Nearest BR station, Bangor
On site facilities: The castle is open to the public, and contains a gift shop. Light refreshments are available
Public opening: Daily 1 April-31 October.
Special notes: For those interested in stately homes the castle is well worth a visit. The entrance fee covers both the castle and the railway exhibits housed in the castle courtyard

Industrial locomotives

Name	No	Builder	Type	Built
Kettering Furnaces No 3	—	B/Hawthorn (859)	0-4-0ST	1883
Watkin	—	de Winton	0-4-0VBT	1893
Fire Queen	—	Horlock	0-4-0	1848
Hawarden	—	H/Clarke (526)	0-4-0ST	1899
Vesta	—	H/Clarke (1223)	0-6-0T	1916
Charles	—	Hunslet (283)	0-4-0ST	1882
Hugh Napier	—	Hunslet (855)	0-4-0ST	1904
—	1	Neilson (1561)	0-4-0WT	1870
Haydock	—	Stephenson (3209)	0-6-0T	1879

Stock
7 narrow gauge rolling stock exhibits from the Padarn/Penrhyn system.
The small relics section includes a comprehensive display of railway signs.

Below: Fire Queen *seen here at Dinorwic slate quarries, prior to removal to Penrhyn Castle Museum.* *K. A. Jaggers*

Caerphilly Railway Society

Location: Harold Wilson Industrial Estate
Operating society/organisation: Caerphilly Railway Society Ltd, Harold Wilson Industrial Estate, Van Road, Caerphilly, Mid-Glamorgan
Car park: At the site
On site facilities: There is a souvenir shop and light refreshments are available.
Public opening: Every Sunday 14.00-17.00. Steam rides are available on open days

Locomotives

Name	*No*	*Origin*	*Class*	*Type*	*Built*
—	41312	BR	2MT	2-6-2T	1952
—	28	TVR	01	0-6-2T	1897

Industrial locomotives

Name	*No*	*Builder*	*Type*	*Built*
Victory	—	Barclay (2201)	0-4-0ST	1945
Forester	—	Barclay (1260)	0-4-0ST	1911
Desmond	—	Avonside (1498)	0-4-0ST	1906
—	—	RSH (7705)	0-4-0ST	1952

Stock
2 freight wagons
1 ex-BR Mk1 coach.
1 staff and tool van

Owner
28 (the National Museum of Wales)

Below: ***Ivatt 2-6-2T No 41312 soon after arrival.*** G. F. Scott-Lowe

North Norfolk Railway

Headquarters: North Norfolk Railway, Sheringham station, Sheringham Norfolk, NR26 8RA.
Telephone: Sheringham 822045
Main station: Sheringham
Other public stations: Weybourne
Car parks: Sheringham (old goods yard), Weybourne
Access by public transport: Sheringham BR station (200 yards)
Refreshment facilities: Sheringham, Weybourne
Souvenir shops: Sheringham, Weybourne
Museum: Sheringham
Depot: Weybourne
Passenger trains: Steeply graded, Sheringham-Weybourne (3 miles)
Period of public operation: Saturdays June-September. Sundays April-October. Tuesdays, Wednesdays (Wednesdays May-September) Thursdays July-August
Special Notes: Not all the stock is located on the line, but is in store at various sites in East Anglia

Locomotives

Name	*No*	*Origin*	*Class*	*Type*	*Built*
—	564	GER	J15	0-6-0	1912
—	61572	LNER	B12	4-6-0	1928

Industrial locomotives

Name	*No*	*Builder*	*Type*	*Built*
Pony	—	H/Leslie (2918)	0-4-0ST	1912
Ring Haw	—	Hunslet (1982)	0-6-0ST	1940
Harlaxton	—	Barclay (2107)	0-6-0T	1941
—	4	Bagnall (2680)	0-6-0ST	1944
John D Hamer	5	Peckett (1970)	0-6-0ST	1939
—	12	RSH (7845)	0-6-0T	1955
Colwyn	45	Kitson (5470)	0-6-0ST	1933
Dr Harry	—	Fowler (410001)	4wDM	1945
—	10	E/Electric	260hp DH	—
—	4	Fowler	4wDM	1953

Stock
2 WMB ex-BR diesel railbuses
4 ex-BR Mk1 coaches
2 ex-SR 'Brighton Belle' Pullman cars
7 ex-LNER coaches
2 ex-LMS coaches
Small number of wagons

Owners
564 (the Midland and Great Northern Railway Society)
61572 (the Midland and Great Northern Railway Society)

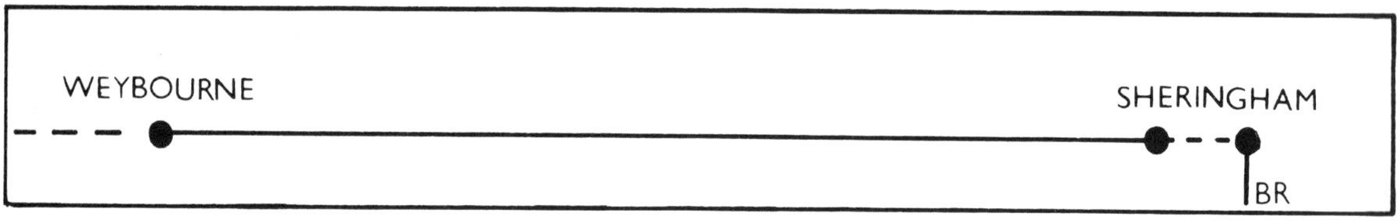

Below: ***Ex-GER 0-6-0 No 564 heads a short freight train away from Weybourne on the North Norfolk Railway.*** *Brian Fisher*

Nene Valley Ra…

Headquarters: Nene Valley Railway, Wansford station, Old North Road, Stibbington, Wansford, near Peterborough, Cambs
Telephone: Stamford 782021/782854
Main station: Wansford
Other public stations: Orton Mere, Ferry Meadows
Car park: Wansford
Access by public transport: Buses from Peterborough to Orton Mere and Ferry Meadows
Refreshment facilities: Wansford
Souvenir shops: Wansford, Orton Mere, Ferry Meadows
Museum: Wansford
Depot: Wansford
Passenger trains: Wansford-Orton Mere ($5\frac{1}{2}$ miles)
Period of public operation: Weekends April-September and Bank Holidays, Wednesdays and Thursdays mid-July-August

Above: ***The Swedish 2-6-2T departs Wansford laying down a thick smoke screen*** *John Titlow*

Locomotives

Name	*No*	*Origin*	*Class*	*Type*	*Built*
—	656	DSR	F	0-6-0T	1949
—	1178	SJ	S	2-6-2T	1914
—	1928	SJ	S1	2-6-4T	1953
—	3.628	SNCF	230D	4-6-0	1911
92 Squadron	34081	SR	BB	4-6-2	1948
City of Peterborough	73050	BR	5MT	4-6-0	1954
—	064-305-6	DB	64	2-6-2T	1936

Industrial locomotives

Name	*No*	*Builder*	*Type*	*Built*
RS16 Fred	—	Avonside (1908)	0-4-0ST	1923
Pitsford	—	Avonside (1917)	0-6-0ST	1923
—	—	Avonside (1945)	0-6-0ST	1926
—	90432	Barclay (2248)	0-4-0ST	1948
—	16	H/Leslie (3835)	0-6-0ST	1934
Derek Crouch	—	H/Clarke (1539)	0-6-0ST	1924
—	—	H/Clarke (1604)	0-6-0ST	1928
Thomas	—	H/Clarke (1800)	0-6-0T	1947
Jacks Green	—	Hunslet (1953)	0-6-0ST	1939
—	75006	Hunslet (2855)	0-6-0ST	1943
—	—	Peckett (2000)	0-6-0ST	1942

Stock
Ex-SR 4-COR electric unit and two other ex-EMU vehicles
Various European coaches

Owners
34081 (the Battle of Britain Locomotive Preservation Society)
73050 (Peterborough City Council)
3.628 (the Nord Locomotive Preservation Group)
Ex-SR electric stock (the Southern Electric Group).

Great Central Railway

Headquarters: Great Central Railway, (Main Line Steam Trust Ltd), Loughborough Central station, Great Central Road, Loughborough, Leicestershire
Telephone: Loughborough 216433 (Saturdays, Sundays), 30726 (other times)
Main station: Loughborough Central
Other public stations: Quorn & Woodhouse, Rothley
Car park: Quorn
Access by public transport: Loughborough BR station ($\frac{3}{4}$ mile). Trent, South Notts & Midland Red bus services to Loughborough bus station ($\frac{3}{4}$ mile)
Refreshment facilities: Gresley buffet car on all trains. Lunches on midday trains Sats & Suns. Light refreshments all day. Dinner trains alternate Sat nights in summer. Refreshment buffet at Loughborough.
Souvenir shop: Loughborough
Museum: Loughborough
Depot: Loughborough Central
Passenger trains: Loughborough-Rothley ($5\frac{1}{2}$ miles)
Special event: Road-Rail-Steam '80. Quorn & Woodhouse station Easter Sunday & Monday.
Period of public operation: Weekends and Bank Holidays, Wednesdays and Thursdays, July and August

Above: *'B1' 4-6-0 No 1306* **Mayflower** *makes a fine sight crossing Swithland Reservoir on the Great Central Railway.* A. R. Kaye

Locomotives

Name	*No*	*Origin*	*Class*	*Type*	*Built*
King Haakon VII	377	NSB	—	2-6-0	1919
Butler Henderson	506	GCR	'Director'	4-4-0	1919
—	985	NER	Y4	0-4-0T	1923
—	5224	GWR	4200	2-8-0T	1924
Witherslack Hall	6990	GWR	'Hall'	4-6-0	1948
*	5231	LMS	5MT	4-6-0	1936
—	61264	LNER	B1	4-6-0	1947
Mayflower	1306	LNER	B1	4-6-0	1948
—	4744	LNER	N2	0-6-2T	1921
Boscastle	34039	SR	WC	4-6-2	1946
Duke of Gloucester	71000	BR	8P	4-6-2	1954

*No5231 is named *3rd (Volunteer) Battalion The Worcestershire and Sherwood Foresters Regiment*

Industrial locomotives

Name	*No*	*Builder*	*Type*	*Built*
Lamport No 3	—	Bagnall (2670)	0-6-0ST	1942
Marston No 3	—	H/Leslie (3581)	0-4-0ST	1924
Robert Nelson	4	Hunslet (1800)	0-6-0ST	1936
Littleton No 5	—	M/Wardle (2018)	0-6-0ST	1922
—	39	RSH (6947)	0-6-0T	1938
Hilda	—	Peckett (1963)	0-4-0ST	1938

Owners

506 (on loan from the National Railway Museum)
985 (the Y7 Locomotive Society)
4744 (the Gresley Society)
6990 (the Witherslack Hall Locomotive Society)
61264 (the Thompson B1 Locomotive Society)
71000 (the Duke of Gloucester Steam Locomotive Trust)

Market Bosworth Light Railway

Headquarters: Market Bosworth Light Railway, Shackerstone station, near Market Bosworth, Leicestershire.
Telephone: Atherstone 3966 (General Manager)
Main station: Shackerstone
Other public station: Market Bosworth
Car park: Shackerstone
Access by public transport: Bus to Market Bosworth (Square) from Leicester (daily). Hinckley and Coalville (not Sundays)
Refreshment facilities: Shackerstone
Souvenir shop: Shackerstone
Museum: Shackerstone
Depot: Shackerstone
Passenger trains: Shackerstone-Market Bosworth ($2\frac{3}{4}$ miles)
Special notes: Market Bosworth Light Railway is operated by members of Shackerstone Railway Society Ltd, with the financial support of York Caravan Equipments Ltd, Atherstone. *Florence No 2* is on long term loan from National Coal Board. An extension of the line from Market Bosworth to Shenton is being undertaken
Period of public operation: Sundays and Bank Holidays Easter-October and Wednesdays only July and August

Locomotives

Name	*No*	*Origin*	*Class*	*Type*	*Built*
—	78018	BR	2MT	2-6-0	1954
—	D2245	BR	04	0-6-0DM	1956

Industrial locomotives

Name	*No*	*Builder*	*Type*	*Built*
Dunlop No 6	—	Bagnall (2648)	0-4-0ST	1941
The King	—	Borrows (48)	0-4-0WT	1906
—	21	H/Leslie (3931)	0-6-0ST	1938
—	11	Hunslet (1493)	0-4-0ST	1925
Dunlop No 7	—	Peckett (2130)	0-4-0ST	1951
Herbert	—	Peckett (2012)	0-4-0ST	1942
—	3	RSH (7537)	0-6-0T	1949
—	4	RSH (7684)	0-6-0T	1951
Florence No2	—	Bagnall (3059)	0-6-0ST	1954
Peeping Tom	—	R/Hornsby (235513)	4wDM	1945

Stock
3 ex-BR Mk1 coaches
2 ex-BR converted dmu coaches
2 rail mounted steam cranes
1 rail mounted diesel crane
Small number of wagons

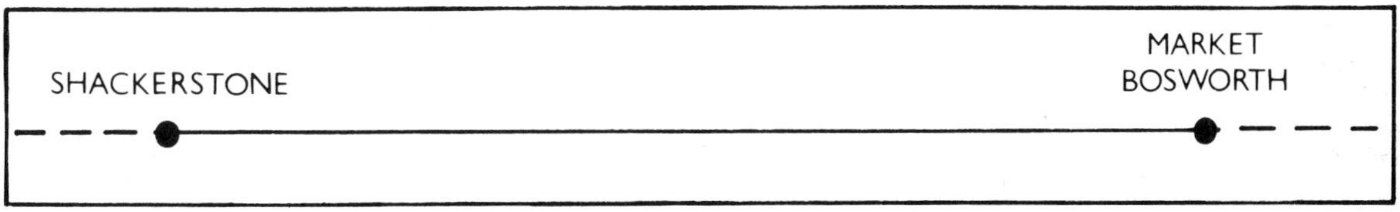

Chappel Steam Centre

Location: Chappel Steam Centre, Chappel & Wakes Colne station
Operating society/organisation: Stour Valley Railway Preservation Society, Chappel & Wakes Colne station, Essex
Car park: Chappel
Access by public transport: Chappel & Wakes Colne BR station
On site facilities: Light refreshments, and bookshop
Public opening: Every weekend 11.00-18.00
Special notes: Special steam days are held during summer months

Locomotives

Name	*No*	*Origin*	*Class*	*Type*	*Built*
—	999	GER	N7	0-6-2T	1924
—	80151	BR	4MT	2-6-4T	1956

Industrial locomotives

Name	*No*	*Builder*	*Type*	*Built*
Jubilee	—	Bagnall (2541)	0-4-0ST	1936
—	1074	Barclay (1047)	0-4-0ST	1905
Belvoir	—	Barclay (2305)	0-6-0ST	1954
Gunby	68067	Hunslet (2413)	0-6-0ST	1941
—	2	M/Vick	0-4-0E	1912
—	—	M/Rail (2029)	4wPM	1920
—	54	RSH (7013)	0-6-0ST	1941
Jupiter	—	RSH (7671)	0-6-0T	1950
—	—	RSH (7597)	0-6-0T	1949
—	—	RSH (7846)	0-6-0T	1955

Stock
9 ex-LNER coaches
1 ex-BR Mk1 coach
1 GER 6-wheel full brake
1 GER 4-wheel coach
1 GER 6-wheel coach
Small number of wagons

Bressingham Steam Museum

Location: Two miles west of Diss on the A1066
Operating society/organisation: Bressingham Steam Museum Trust, Bressingham Hall, Diss, Norfolk
Telephone: Bressingham 386
Car park: Steam Centre (free)
Access by public transport: Diss BR station (3 miles). Bus meets 10.30 train from Liverpool Street
On site facilities: $9\frac{1}{2}$/15/24in and standard gauge lines, totalling nearly 5 miles. Museum, steam roundabout and street organ
Public opening: Thursdays late May-mid September 13.30-17.30. Sundays and Bank holidays from early May-late September, 13.30-18.00. Wednesdays during August 13.30-17.30
Special notes: Reduced rates for coach parties

Locomotives

Name	*No*	*Origin*	*Class*	*Type*	*Built*
Martello	62	LBSCR	A1X	0-6-0T	1875
Thundersley	80	LTSR	3P	4-4-2T	1909
—	102	LSWR	B4	0-4-0T	1893
—	1217E	GER	J17	0-6-0	1905
—	2500	LMS	4MT	2-6-4T	1934
Royal Scot	6100	LMS	7P	4-6-0	1927
Duchess of Sutherland	6233	LMS	8P	4-6-2	1938
Oliver Cromwell	70013	BR	7MT	4-6-2	1951
—	5865	NSB	52	2-10-0	1944
—	141R73	SNCF	141R	2-8-2	1945

Industrial locomotives

Name	*No*	*Builder*	*Type*	*Built*
—	1	Neilson (4444)	0-4-0WT	1892
—	25	Neilson (5087)	0-4-0ST	1896
Solomon	4	M/Wardle (641)	0-6-0ST	1877
—	6841	B/Peacock (6841)	0-4-4-0	1937
Millfield	—	RSH (7070)	0-4-0CT	1942

Narrow gauge locomotives

Gwynedd	—	Hunslet (316)	0-4-0ST	1937
George Sholto	—	Hunslet (994)	0-4-0ST	1909
Bronllwyd	—	H/Clarke (1643)	0-6-0WT	1930
Bronhilde	—	Schwartzkopf (9124)	0-4-0WT	1927
Eigiau	—	O&K (5668)	0-4-0WT	1912
—	—	R&H (437367)	4wDM	1959

Below: ***'Royal Scot' class 4-6-0 No 6100* Royal Scot *seen at the Bressingham Steam Museum in July 1977.*** C. J. Tults

Above: Mannertreu *on Bressingham's 15in gauge Waveney Valley Railway.* *C. J. Tuffs*

15in gauge locomotives

Rosenkavalier	—	Krupp (1662)	4-6-2	1937
Mannertreu	—	Krupp (1663)	4-6-2	1937

9½in gauge locomotives

Princess	—	Motor Gear & Engine Co	4-6-2	1947

Owners
62 (Butlins)
80 (on loan from the National Railway Museum)
102 (Butlins)
1217E (on loan from the National Railway Museum)
2500 (on loan from the National Railway Museum)
6100 (Butlins)
6233 (Butlins)
70013 (on loan from the National Railway Museum)

Colne Valley Railway

Location: Castle Hedingham station, Yeldham Road, Castle Hedingham, Halstead, Essex
Operating society/organisation: Colne Valley Railway Preservation Society
Telephone: Hedingham 61174
Car park: At the site (access from A604 road)
Access by public transport: Eastern National bus services No 88 Colchester-Halstead, 89 Halstead-Hedingham and Hedingham & District Nos 4 Braintree-Hedingham, 5 Sudbury-Hedingham.
On site facilities: Depot, museum, souvenir shop and refreshments
Public opening: Daily for static displays. Locomotives in steam once per month during summer season, as advertised, and all bank holidays except Christmas & New Year
Special notes: The railway has been completely rebuilt on part of the original Colne Valley line track-bed

Industrial locomotives

Name	*No*	*Builder*	*Type*	*Built*
Victory	—	Barclay (2199)	0-4-0ST	1945
Castle Hedingham	—	Hunslet (3790)	0-6-0ST	1952
—	72	Vulcan (5309)	0-6-0ST	1945
—	40	RSH (7765)	0-6-0T	1954
Barrington	—	Avonside (1875)	0-4-0ST	1921
—	1	H/Leslie (3715)	0-4-0ST	1928

Stock
1 ex-BR Mk1 coach and sundry items of freight stock.
1 ex-Norwegian State Railway Class B 65 No 18803 (built 1926) Balcony Open Second (teak)

Crich Tramway Museum

Location: Crich, near Matlock, Derbyshire DE4 5DP
Operating society/organisation: Tramway Museum Society
Telephone: 077 385 2565
Car park: Site, coach parking also available
Access by public transport: Trent bus services Nos 240/1. Nearest stations: Matlock (BR) or Alfreton & Mansfield Parkway (BR) then by bus; or Whatstandwell (BR) and steep uphill walk
On site facilities: Souvenir shop, cafe and picnic area. 1 mile electric tramway.
Public opening: Saturdays, Sundays and Bank holidays from April-October (10.30-17.00). Also Tuesdays-Thursdays mid-May-August 10.00-16.30. Admission Adults £1, children 50p (including return tram ride) except August Bank Holiday
Special Notes: Crich houses the largest collection of preserved trams in Europe and has a 1 mile working tramway on which restored trams are operated. Annual 'Transport Extravaganzas' are held, when other vintage vehicles are present and special events are arranged. Part of tram line occupies route of narrow gauge mineral railway built by George Stephenson

Locomotives

Name	*No*	*Builder*	*Type*	*Built*
—	—	B/Peacock (2464)	0-4-0VB tram loco	1885
—	—	E/Electric	4wE	1927
Rupert	—	R/Hornsby (223741)	4wD	1944
GMJ	—	R/Hornsby (326058)	4wD	1952
—	—	R/Hornsby (373363)	4wD	1954

Also some 40 trams including examples from Czechoslovakia, Portugal and South Africa, about half of which have been restored to working order.

Above: ***Beyer Peacock 0-4-0VB tram loco and other exhibits at the Crich Tramway Museum*** *J. A. Price*

Midland Railway Centre

Location: Midland Railway Centre, Butterley station, near Ripley, Derbyshire
Operating society/organisation: Midland Railway Trust Ltd
Telephone: Ripley 44920
Car park: Butterley station on A61 1 mile north of Ripley
On site facilities: Refreshments, souvenir shop, display vehicles and exhibition coach
Public opening: Every Saturday and Sunday from April-October, 10.00-dusk. Also open on Bank Holiday Mondays
Special notes: This centre is being established as a working museum of Midland Railway practice, which will eventually include a double track running line with stations built in original style

Locomotives

Name	*No*	*Origin*	*Class*	*Type*	*Built*
—	73129	BR	5MT	4-6-0	1956
Princess Margaret Rose	6203	LMS	8P	4-6-2	1935
—	44027	LMS	4F	0-6-0	1924
—	47564	LMS	3F	0-6-0T	1928
—	47327	LMS	3F	0-6-0T	1926
—	16440	LMS	3F	0-6-0T	1926
—	47445	LMS	3F	0-6-0T	1927
—	158A	MR	—	2-4-0	1866
—	673	MR	—	4-2-2	1897
—	1708	MR	1F	0-6-0T	1880
—	12077	BR		0-6-0DE	1950

Industrial locomotives

Name	*No*	*Builder*	*Type*	*Built*
Gladys	—	Markham (109)	0-4-0ST	1894
Stanton	24	Barclay (1875)	0-4-0CT	1925
Victory	—	Peckett (1547)	0-4-0ST	1917
—	BB No 4	Nasmyth Wilson	0-4-0ST	1894
—	—	Sentinel (9632)	4wVB	1956
Andy	—	Fowler (16038)	0-4-0D	1923
—	2271	Drewry (2615)	0-6-0D	1958
*Handyman**	—	H/Clarke (573)	0-4-0ST	1900
—	RS9	M/Rail (2024)	0-4-0D	1921
—	RS12	M/Rail (460)	0-4-0D	1912
—	—	M/Rail (1930)	0-4-0P	1919
—	2	Fowler (20685)	2-4-0D	1935

Owners
6203 (Butlins)
1708 (the 1708 Locomotive Preservation Trust)
16440 (the Derby Council)
44027 (on loan from the National Railway Museum)
47327 (Derbyshire County Council)
47445 (Derbyshire County Council)
47564 (Derbyshire County Council)
73129 (Derbyshire County Council)

*3ft gauge

Below: *'4F' 0-6-0 No 44027 and Caprotti Class '5MT' 4-6-0 No 73129 at Butterley.* *B. Morrison*

WEST MIDLANDS

Severn Valley Railway

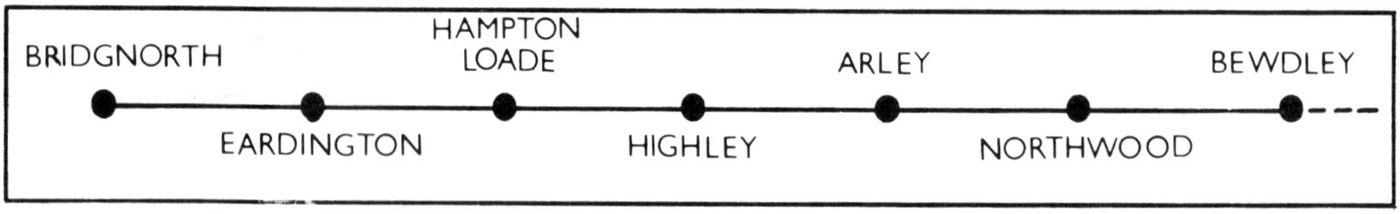

Headquarters: The Railway Station, Bewdley, Worcestershire
Telephone: Bewdley 403816
Main stations: Bridgnorth, Bewdley
Other public stations: Arley, Highley, Hampton Loade, Eardington, Northwood Halt
Car parks: Bridgnorth, Bewdley. Limited parking at all stations
Access by public transport: Midland Red bus services Nos X92 to Bewdley, 890 to Bridgnorth
Refreshment facilities: Bridgnorth, Bewdley, and on most trains.
Souvenir shops: Bridgnorth, Bewdley.
Depot: Bridgnorth (locomotives), Bewdley. (stock)
Passenger trains: Steam-hauled trains Bridgnorth-Bewdley ($12\frac{1}{2}$ miles). Services extended from Bewdley to Foley Park, Kidderminster on enthusiasts' weekends.
Period of public operation: Weekends March-October and December. Weekdays during May, June, July-August and at Bank Holidays
Special notes: A number of special enthusiasts' weekends are held when extra trains are operated and special events are held. In addition supplementary trains with diesel haulage may be run on special occasions.
BR dmu connecting service between Bewdley and Kidderminster may operate during 1980

Left: *GWR 0-6-0 No 3205 storms out of Bridgnorth in 1970, this locomotive will re-enter service this year after a rebuild.* *Paul Cotterell*

Locomotives

Name	*No*	*Origin*	*Class*	*Type*	*Built*
Great Marquess	3442	LNER	K4	2-6-0	1938
Gordon	AD600	LMR	WD	2-10-0	1943
—	43106	LMS	4MT	2-6-0	1951
—	6443	LMS	2MT	2-6-0	1950
—	46521	LMS	2MT	2-6-0	1953
—	5000	LMS	5MT	4-6-0	1934
RAF Biggin Hill	45110	LMS	5MT	4-6-0	1935
—	47383	LMS	3F	0-6-0	1926
—	8233	LMS	8F	2-8-0	1940
—	2968	LMS	5P4F	2-6-0	1933
—	3205	GWR	2251	0-6-0	1946
—	2857	GWR	2800	2-8-0	1918
—	5164	GWR	5101	2-6-2T	1930
—	4150	GWR	5101	2-6-2T	1947
—	4141	GWR	5101	2-6-2T	1946
—	5764	GWR	5700	0-6-0PT	1929
—	7714	GWR	5700	0-6-0PT	1930
Raveningham Hall	6960	GWR	'Hall'	4-6-0	1944
—	4566	GWR	4500	2-6-2T	1924
Hinton Manor	7819	GWR	'Manor'	4-6-0	1939
Erlestoke Manor	7812	GWR	'Manor'	4-6-0	1939
Britannia	70000	BR	7MT	4-6-2	1951
Hagley Hall	4930	GWR	'Hall'	4-6-0	1929
—	1501	GWR	1500	0-6-0PT	1949
—	9303	GWR	4300	2-6-0	1932
—	80079	BR	4MT	2-6-4T	1954
—	78019	BR	2MT	2-6-0	1954
—	75069	BR	4MT	4-6-0	1955
Western Ranger	D1013	BR	52	C-C	1962
Western Courier	D1062	BR	52	C-C	1963

Industrial locomotives

Name	*No*	*Builder*	*Type*	*Built*
Shropshire	193	Hunslet (3793)	0-6-0ST	1953
—	4	Peckett (1738)	0-4-0ST	1928
Highflyer	—	Fowler (22912)	0-4-0D	1940
Mary	—	H/Clarke	0-4-0D	1932
—	813	H/Clarke (555)	0-6-0ST	1901
Warwickshire	—	M/Wardle (2047)	0-6-0ST	1926
The Lady Armaghdale	—	Hunslet (686)	0-6-0T	1898

Stock
25 ex-GWR coaches
11 ex-LMS coaches
11 ex-BR Mk 1 coaches
7 other coaches
Numerous examples of ex-GWR, LMS and other freight vehicles

Owners
813 (the 813 Preservation Fund)
1501 (the Warwickshire Railway Society)
2857 (the Severn Valley Railway 2857 Society)
4150 (the Severn Valley Railway 4150 Locomotive Fund)
7812 (the Erlestoke Manor Fund)
9303 (the Great Western (SVR) Association)
2968 (the Stanier Mogul Fund)
5000 (on loan from the National Railway Museum)
47383 (the Manchester Rail Travel Society)
8233 (the Stanier 8F Locomotive Society)
70000 (the Britannia Locomotive Society)
D1062 (the 'Western' locomotive Association)

Foxfield Light Railway

Headquarters: Foxfield Light Railway, Dilhorne, Blythe Bridge, Stoke on Trent.
Telephone: Uttoxeter 4669
Main station: Foxfield Dilhorne station
Car park: Foxfield
Access by public transport: Potteries Motor Traction bus service No 86B from Longton or Cheadle, alighting at Godley Brook, 200yds from Foxfield station.
Refreshment facilities: Foxfield
Souvenir shop: Foxfield
Passenger trains: Steam-hauled trains operate from Foxfield to Cash Heath (3 miles)
Period of public operation: Sundays and Bank Holidays only, April-September. Special trains at other times by prior arrangement

Industrial locomotives

Name	*No*	*Builder*	*Type*	*Built*
Wimblebury	—	Hunslet (3839)	0-6-0ST	1956
Roker	—	RSH (7006)	0-4-0CT	1940
—	35	M/Wardle (1317)	0-6-0ST	1895
Robert	—	Avonside (2068)	0-6-0ST	1933
Cranford	—	Avonside (1919)	0-6-0ST	1924
Topham	—	Bagnall (2193)	0-6-0ST	1922
Lewisham	—	Bagnall (2221)	0-6-0ST	1927
J. T. Daly	—	Bagnall (2450)	0-4-0ST	1931
Hawarden	—	Bagnall (2623)	0-4-0ST	1940
Henry Cort	—	Peckett (933)	0-4-0ST	1903
—	11	Peckett (2081)	0-4-0ST	1947
—	1	Barclay (1984)	0-4-0F	1930
—	—	Simplex (2262)	4wD	1924
—	—	Sentinel (9535)	0-4-0	1952

Stock
3 coaches
4 scenery vans
13 wagons
1 steam crane

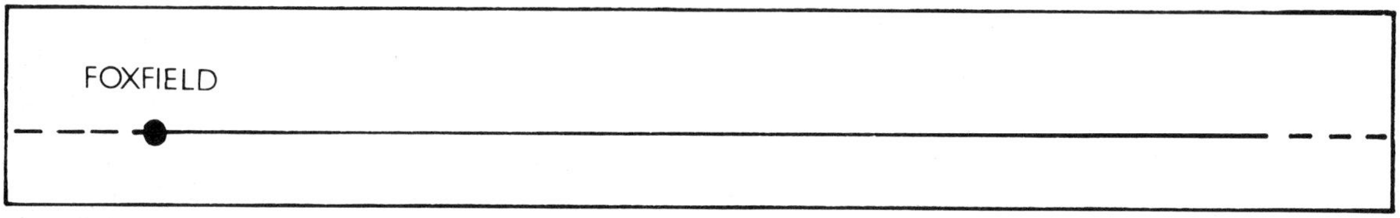

Chasewater Light Railway

Location: Chasewater Pleasure Park, Brownhills, West Midlands
Operating society/organisation: Chasewater Light Railway Society
Telephone: 021 355 3812 (Hon Sec) Railway Brownhills 5852
Car park: Pleasure park
Access by public transport: Midland Red bus services Nos 853 and 854 from Birmingham and Cannock 345 and 394 from Birmingham
On site facilities: Refreshments, museum and souvenir shop. Passenger train service available on specified occasions. Extensive small relics collection.
Public opening: April-September, second and fourth Sundays in each month, plus Bank holiday Sundays and Mondays. Steam trains operate from 14.00
Special notes: Trains available for hire to groups booking in advance

Industrial locomotives

Name	*No*	*Builder*	*Type*	*Built*
—	—	Peckett (917)	0-4-0ST	1902
—	—	Barclay (2220)	0-4-0ST	1946
—	—	Barclay (1223)	0-4-0ST	1911
The Colonel	—	Peckett (1351)	0-4-0ST	1914
Alfred Paget	11	Neilson (2937)	0-4-0ST	1882
—	S100	H/Clarke (1822)	0-6-0T	1949
—	15	H/Clarke (431)	0-6-0ST	1895
Asbestos	—	H/Leslie (2780)	0-4-0ST	1909
—	1	Planet (2914)	4wD	1944
—	20	Kent/Planet	4wD	1926
—	21	Kent/Planet (1612)	4wD	1929
—	DL7	R/Hornsby	0-4-0D	1961
—	—	Smiths	4wD crane	1951

Stock
Passenger services provided with an ex-BR dmu trailer car.
A selection of freight vehicles is also housed at the site, also several pre-Grouping coaches.

Birmingham Railway Museum

Location: The Steam Depot, Warwick Road, Birmingham.
Operating society/organisation: Standard Gauge Steam Trust
Car park: Site (except on Steam Days)
Access by public transport: WMPTE bus routes Nos 37, 44 from city centre
On site facilities: This former BR motive power depot has been equipped with much specialised railway engineering machinery. Souvenir Shop. Relics shop, buffet car (mid 1980)
Public opening: Static display every Sunday 14.00-17.30. Closed on Bank holidays. Steam Days on first Sunday of each month April-December (except August) 11.00-17.30
Special notes: Tyseley is a centre for 'Steam on BR' railtours over the BR lines to Stratford upon Avon and Didcot (via Oxford). Development plans envisage the construction of a roundhouse small exhibits museum, station and other ancillary features over the next 10 years financed by a Development Trust backed by Industry. The Museum is partly owned by the West Midlands County Council

Above: *No 7029* Clun Castle *ascends the Lickey incline while returning to the Birmingham Railway Museum at Tyseley after working a main line steam special.* *R. E. B. Siviter*

Locomotives

Name	*No*	*Origin*	*Class*	*Type*	*Built*
Albert Hall	4983	GWR	'Hall'	4-6-0	1931
Earl of Mount Edgcumbe	5043	GWR	'Castle'	4-6-0	1936
Defiant	5080	GWR	'Castle'	4-6-0	1939
Thornbury Castle	7027	GWR	'Castle'	4-6-0	1949
Clun Castle	7029	GWR	'Castle'	4-6-0	1950
—	5637	GWR	5600	0-6-2T	1925
—	7752	GWR	5700	0-6-0PT	1930
—	7760	GWR	5700	0-6-0PT	1930
—	9600	GWR	5700	0-6-0PT	1945
—	4160	GWR	5101	2-6-2T	1948
Kolhapur	5593	LMS	'Jubilee'	4-6-0	1934

Industrial locomotives

Name	*No*	*Builder*	*Type*	*Built*
Rocket	—	Peckett (1722)	0-4-0ST	1926
—	1	Peckett (2004)	0-4-0ST	1942

Stock
4 Pullman cars
1 Gresley buffet car
1 LNWR semi Royal Saloon
1 GWR semi Royal Saloon
1 30ton steam crane and sundry goods vehicles

Owners
4983 (the 4983 Albert Hall Ltd)
5637 (the 4983 Albert Hall Ltd)
5080 (for spare parts only)

Bulmer Railway Centre

Location: H. P. Bulmer Ltd (Cider Makers), Whitecross Road, Hereford. The site is $\frac{1}{4}$ mile from city centre on A438 Hereford-Brecon road
Operating society: The 6000 Locomotive Association in conjunction with the Merchant Navy Locomotive Preservation Society and the Princess Elizabeth Locomotive Society, on behalf of H. P. Bulmer Ltd
Telephone: Hereford 6182
Car park: At the site
Access by public transport: Midland Red bus services Nos H1, H3, H11 and Yeoman's Hereford-Kington & Credenhill bus services. Hereford (BR) station (1 mile)
On site facilities: Sales. Refreshment facilities on steam open days only
Public opening: 5 April-28 September, static displays on weekends only. Brakevan rides behind *Pectin* on last Sunday in each month. Steam Open Days on Easter Sunday and Monday, Spring Bank Holiday Sunday and Monday and last Sunday in September — main line locos in steam and other attractions. 11.00-17.00
Special notes: Hereford is a centre for 'Steam on BR' railtours over BR mainlines

Locomotives

Name	*No*	*Origin*	*Class*	*Type*	*Built*
King George V	6000	GWR	'King'	4-6-0	1927
—	5786	GWR	5700	0-6-0PT	1930
Clan Line	35028	SR	MN	4-6-2	1948
Princess Elizabeth	6201	LMS	7P	4-6-2	1933

Industrial locomotives

Name	*No*	*Builder*	*Type*	*Built*
Cider Queen	2	Hunslet (6999)	0-6-0D	1955
Pectin	—	Peckett (1579)	0-4-0ST	1921
Woodpecker	—	Fowler(22871)	0-4-0D	1939
Carnarvon	47	Kitson (5474)	0-6-0ST	1934

Stock

H. P. Bulmer 'Cider Train' consisting of five Pullman cars converted for exhibition purposes
Several ex-BR Mk1 coaches
Pullman car from ex-SR 6-PUL electric unit
Small number of freight vehicles

Owners

6201 (the Princess Elizabeth Locomotive Society)
35028 (the Merchant Navy Locomotive Preservation Society)

Below: ***The three main line locomotives at Bulmer Railway Centre have all seen considerable service on BR main line steam railtours.*** *Ian Allan Library*

Ironbridge Gorge Museum

Location: Ironbridge, Shropshire
Operating society/organisation: Ironbridge Gorge Museum Trust, Ironbridge, Telford, Shropshire TF8 7AW
Telephone: Ironbridge (095 245) 3522
Car park: At the site
Access by public transport: Midland Red bus services to Ironbridge
Public opening: Daily (10.00-18.00) April-October. Daily (10.00-17.00) November-March. Closed Christmas Day
Special notes: Combined tickets to the various museums are available. At some sites no charge is made

Locomotives

Name	*No*	*Builder*	*Type*	*Date*
—	—	Sentinel/Coalbrookdale (6185)	0-4-0VBT	1925*
—	—	Sentinel/M/Wardle (6155)	0-4-0VBT	1925*
—	5	Coalbrookdale	0-4-0ST	1865†
Peter	—	Barclay (782)	0-6-0ST	1896

*At Museum of Iron, Coalbrookdale
†At Blists Hill Open Air Museum

Telford Horsehay Steam Trust

Location: Horsehay, Telford
Operating society/organisation: Telford Horsehay Steam Trust, The Old Loco Shed, Horsehay, Telford
Public opening: Tuesday 19.00-22.00, Saturday 10.00-17.00, Sunday 10.00-13.00

Locomotives

Name	*No*	*Origin*	*Class*	*Type*	*Date*
—	485*	LNWR	G2	0-8-0	1921
—	5619	GWR	5600	0-6-2T	1925

Industrial locomotives

Name	*No*	*Builder*	*Type*	*Date*
Tom	—	N/British (27414)	0-4-0D	1954

Stock
1 ex-GWR auto-trailer

*Stored on behalf of Ironbridge Gorge Museum Trust

North Staffordshire Railway

Location: Cheddleton station, near Leek, Staffordshire
Operating society/organisation: North Staffordshire Railway Company (1978) Ltd
Telephone: Stoke on Trent 503520, Churnet Side 360522
Car park: At the site (30p)
Access by public transport: A regular bus service operates from the Potteries and Leek to Cheddleton village
On site facilities: Include a museum, sales area, lecture rooms and buffet
Public opening: May-September, Monday to Saturday 12.00-17.30, Sundays and Bank Holidays 11.00-18.30. October-April, Sundays only 12.00-17.30. Closed Christmas Day
Special notes: Facilities for the disabled. Coach parties by arrangement

Locomotives

Name	*No*	*Origin*	*Class*	*Type*	*Built*
—	4422	LMS	4F	0-6-0	1927
—	80136	BR	4MT	2-6-4T	1956

Industrial locomotives

Name	*No*	*Builder*	*Type*	*Built*
—	3777	Hunslet (3777)	0-6-0ST	1952

Stock
2 ex-BR Mk1 coaches

Lakeside and Haverthwaite Railway

Headquarters: Haverthwaite station, near Newby Bridge, Ulverston, Cumbria LA12 8AL.
Telephone: Newby Bridge 594
Main station: Haverthwaite
Other public stations: Intermediate station at Newby Bridge. Terminus at Lakeside on Windermere
Car parks: Haverthwaite, Lakeside on Windermere
Access by public transport: Sealink ships on Lake Windermere call at Lakeside. Ribble bus to Haverthwaite
Refreshment facilities: Haverthwaite
Souvenir shop: Haverthwaite
Depot: All rolling stock at Haverthwaite
Passenger trains: Steam-hauled Haverthwaite-Lakeside ($3\frac{1}{2}$miles)
Period of public operation: Easter then daily from early-May to end of September. Sundays only in October.
Special notes: Combined railway/lake steamer tickets available, from the station at Haverthwaite, Ambleside, and Bowness, Piers of Sealink

Locomotives

Name	*No*	*Origin*	*Class*	*Type*	*Built*
—	2073	LMS	4MT	2-6-4T	1950
—	2085	LMS	4MT	2-6-4T	1951
—	8	BR	03	0-6-0DM	1953

Industrial locomotives

Name	*No*	*Builder*	*Type*	*Built*
Caliban	1	Peckett (1925)	0-4-0ST	1937
Fluff	2	Hunslet	0-4-0DM	1937
—	5	H/Clarke (1631)	0-6-0ST	1929
Renishaw Ironworks No 6	6	H/Clarke (1366)	0-6-0ST	1919
Rachel	9	M/Rail	4Wtram	1924
Repulse	11	Hunslet (3698)	0-6-0ST	1950
Princess	14	Bagnall (2682)	0-6-0ST	1942
Askam Hall	12	H/Leslie	0-4-0ST	1935
Alexandra	14	Barclay (929)	0-4-0ST	1902
David	15	Braclay 2333)	0-4-0ST	1953
Cumbria	94	Hunslet (3794)	0-6-0ST	1953

Stock
8 ex-BR Mk1 coaches
1 ex-LNER coach
1 ex-MR coach
Small selection of freight vehicles

Owner
12 (Copeland Borough Council)

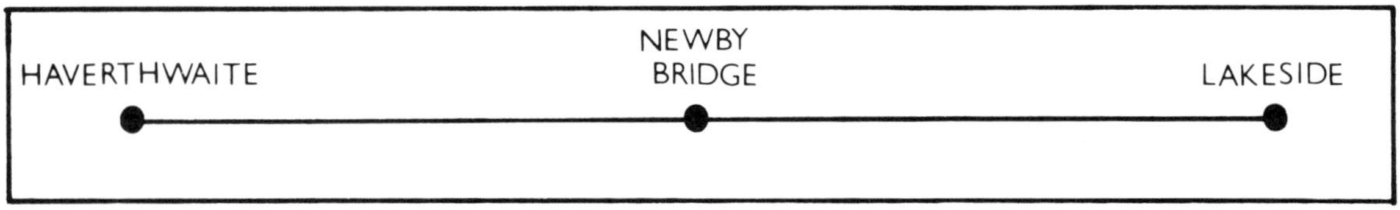

Below: ***Fairburn 2-6-4T No 2085 heads an afternoon train away from Haverthwaite.***
R. D. Clarke

Ravenglass and Eskdale Railway

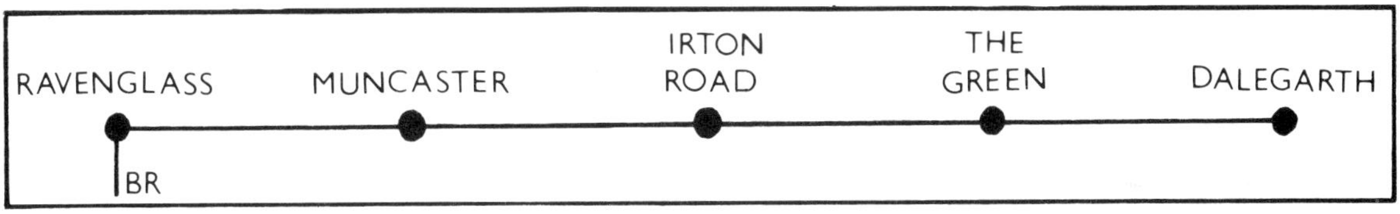

Headquarters: Ravenglass and Eskdale Railway, Ravenglass station, Cumbria
Telephone: 06577 226
Main station: Ravenglass
Other public stations: Muncaster, Irton Road, The Green, Eskdale (Dalegarth)
Car parks: Ravenglass, Dalegarth
Access by public transport: BR services to Ravenglass. CMS buses between Whitehaven and Millom call at Ravenglass
Refreshment facilities: Ravenglass, Dalegarth
Souvenir shops: Ravenglass, Dalegarth
Museum: Ravenglass
Passenger trains: Steam or diesel-hauled (15in) narrow gauge trains Ravenglass-Dalegarth (7 miles)
Period of public operation: Daily from late March-late October. Limited winter service November-March
Special notes: At Ravenglass the R&ER has two camping coaches and the company also operates the 'Ratty Arms' public house formed by conversion of the former BR station buildings

Locomotives

Name	*No*	*Builder*	*Type*	*Built*
River Mite	—	Clarkson (4669)	2-8-2	1966
Northern Rock	—	R&ER	2-6-2	1975
River Irt	—	Heywood	0-8-2	1894
River Esk	—	Davey Paxman (21104)	2-8-2	1923
Shelagh of Eskdale	—	R&ER/Severn-Lamb	4-6-4D	1968
Quarryman	—	Muir-Hill	0-4-0P/Paraffin	1925
—	—	Muir Hill	0-4-2D	1929
Silver Jubilee	—	R&ER	dmu	1977
*Bonny Dundee**	—	K/Stuart	0-4-0	1900
	—	R&ER†	Bo-Bo	1979

*Being rebuilt as 0-4-2
†Under construction

Above: River Esk *starts away from Irton Road on the Ravenglass & Eskdale Railway on 15 April 1979.* *R. E. Ruffell*

Dinting Railway Centre

Location: Dinting Railway Centre Ltd, Dinting, Glossop, Derbyshire
Operating society/organisation: Bahamas Locomotive Society
Telephone: Glossop 5596
Car park: Free parking on site
Access by public transport: BR services to Dinting station and buses Nos 125, 236, 237 and 354
On site facilities: Refreshments and souvenir shop. Picnic area. Miniature steam railway (Bank Holidays)
Public opening: Daily except Christmas and Boxing Day. Locomotives in steam and brakevan rides available Sundays and Bank Holidays from March-October
Special notes: Dinting is a centre for 'Steam on BR' steam-hauled main line railtours

Locomotives

Name	*No*	*Origin*	*Class*	*Type*	*Built*
Bahamas	5596	LMS	'Jubilee'	4-6-0	1935
Scots Guardsman	6115	LMS	'Royal Scot'	4-6-0	1927
—	102	GCR	04	2-8-0	1911
—	1054	LNWR	—	0-6-2T	1888
Blue Peter	532	LNER	A2/3	4-6-2	1948
Bittern	19	LNER	A4	4-6-2	1937

Industrial locomotives

Name	*No*	*Builder*	*Type*	*Built*
Southwick	—	RSH (7069)	0-4-0CT	1942
Warrington	150	RSH (7136)	0-6-0ST	1944
Nunlow	—	H/Clarke (1704)	0-6-0T	1938
—	1883	Avonside (1883)	0-6-0ST	1923
Tiny	—	Barclay (2258)	0-4-0ST	1949
—	—	B/Peacock (2734)	0-4-0VB tram	1886
—	RS8	Avonside/RR (1913)	0-4-0D	1923
Jacob	—	McEwan Platt (680)	Petrol loco	1916

Stock
Sundry freight vehicles

Owners
1054 (the National Trust)
102 (on loan from the National Railway Museum)

Below: *'Jubilee' class 4-6-0 No 5596* **Bahamas** *and Hunslet 0-6-0ST* **Warrington** *on display at Dinting Railway Centre.* *P. A. Hogarth*

Steamtown, Carnforth

Location: Steamtown Railway Museum Ltd, Warton Road, Carnforth, Lancashire. Formerly BR Carnforth motive power depot
Operating society/organisation: Steamtown Railway Musuem Ltd
Telephone: Carnforth 4220
Car park: Free car park on site
Access by public transport: BR services to Carnforth station. Bus services to Carnforth by Ribble and Lancaster Corporation
On site facilities: Model railway, signalbox, collectors' corner, shop, cafe, gardeners' junction, 15in gauge railway
Public opening: Daily 09.00-18.00 except Christmas Day. Locomotives in steam on Bank Holidays, Sundays from Easter-October, and daily during July-August
Special notes: Carnforth is a centre for 'Steam on BR' steam-hauled railtours over BR main lines. Scheduled BR steam hauled excursions during summer season, operate from Carnforth with through connections from main centres

Locomotives

Name	*No*	*Origin*	*Class*	*Type*	*Built*
Flying Scotsman	4472	LNER	A3	4-6-2	1923
Canadian Pacific	35005	SR	MN	4-6-2	1941
Lord Nelson	30850	SR	LN	4-6-0	1926
—	5643	GWR	5600	0-6-2T	1925
Sovereign	44871	LMS	5MT	4-6-0	1945
—	44932	LMS	5MT	4-6-0	1945
—	45407	LMS	5MT	4-6-0	1937
—	6441	LMS	2MT	2-6-0	1950
—	1122	L&Y	—	0-6-0	1896
—	D2381	BR	03	0-6-0	1960
La France	231K22	SNCF	231K	4-6-2	1914
—	01.1104	DB	01	4-6-2	1940
—	80.014	DR	80	0-6-0T	1927

Industrial locomotives

Name	*No*	*Builder*	*Type*	*Built*
—	A6444	Hunslet (2697)	0-6-0DM	1944
John Howe	5	Barclay (1147)	0-4-0ST	1908
Jane Derbyshire	2	Barclay (1969)	0-4-0ST	1929
Coronation	3	Barclay (2134)	0-4-0ST	1942
Glenfield	1	Barclay (880)	0-4-0CT	1902
May	—	Peckett (1370)	0-4-0ST	1915
Trimpell	—	Bagnall (3019)	0-6-0F	1953
Cranford No 2	—	Bagnall (2668)	0-6-0ST	1942
Firefly	—	Hudswell (1864)	0-6-0T	1942
Esso	—	General Electric	Co-Co	1942

Stock
5 pre-Grouping saloon coaches
1 LNER buffet car
3 Pullman cars
Small selection of freight vehicles

Owners
1122 (the Fairclough Corporation)
4498 (the A4 Locomotive Society)
5690 (the Leander Locomotive Ltd)
30850 (on loan from the National Railway Museum)

Below: ***SNCF Pacific No 231K22.***
David Eatwell

Bury Transport Museum

Location: Bury Transport Museum, Castlecroft Road, Bury, Lancashire BL9 0LN
Operating society/organisation: East Lancashire Railway Preservation Society
Telephone: 061 764 7790
Car park: Castlecroft Road and Bolton Street
Access by public transport: BR to Bury (not Sunday). Greater Manchester Transport and Ribbie Motor Services to Bury
On site facilities: Refreshments, only during steam weekends
Public opening: Saturdays and Sundays throughout year. Locomotives in steam only on last Sunday of month, March-September, also Sunday and Monday at Easter, Spring and Summer Bank Holidays
Special notes: Model railway operating on advertised steam days

Locomotives

Name	*No*	*Builder*	*Type*	*Built*
Gothenburg	32	H/Clarke (680)	0-6-0T	1903
—	70	H/Clarke (1464)	0-6-0T	1921
—	945	Barclay (945)	0-4-0ST	1904
—	1	Barclay (1927)	0-4-0ST	1927
MEA No 1	—	RSH (7683)	0-6-0T	1951

2 4-wheel diesel mechanical locomotives

Stock
1 BR Mk1 TSO
1 L&YR coach
Small number of freight vehicles

Steamport, Southport

Location: Five minutes from BR station, via London Street. Behind car park
Operating society/organisation: Southport Locomotive and Transport Museum, Derby Road, Southport PR9 0TY
Telephone: Southport 30693
Car park: Derby Road
Access by public transport: BR station, Merseyrail from Liverpool
On site facilities: Souvenir shop/cafe at weekends. Steam hauled rides in LMS brake vans May-end September, plus special events
Public opening: October-April 14.00-17.00 Weekends. May-September 13.00-17.00 Weekends. Weekdays June-mid September 13.00-17.00. Daily July-August 11.00-17.00
Special notes: Ex-LNER turntable from York

Locomotives

Name	*No*	*Origin*	*Class*	*Type*	*Built*
Magpie	44806	LMS	5MT	4-6-0	1944
—	5193	GWR	5101	2-6-2T	1934
—	47298	LMS	3F	0-6-0T	1924
—	76079	BR	4MT	2-6-0	1957

Industrial locomotives

Name	*No*	*Builder*	*Type*	*Built*
—	5	Peckett (2153)	0-6-0ST	1954
North Western Gas Board	—	Peckett (1999)	0-4-0ST	1941
Waleswood	—	H/Clarke (750)	0-4-0ST	1906
Kingley	—	Hunslet (1954)	0-6-0ST	1939
Persil	—	Fowler (4160001)	0-4-0DM	1952
*Lucy**	—	Avonside (1568)	0-6-0ST	1909
*Efficient**	—	Barclay (1598)	0-4-0ST	1918

Stock
Small selection of rolling stock

Owner
76079 (Frogstone Ltd)
Stock* (Liverpool Locomotive Preservation Group)

Right: ***The Liverpool Locomotive Group's 'Jinty' 0-6-0T No 47298, recently restored to working order at Steamport, Southport.***
E. Wheelwright

NORTH-EAST

Keighley and Worth Valley Railway

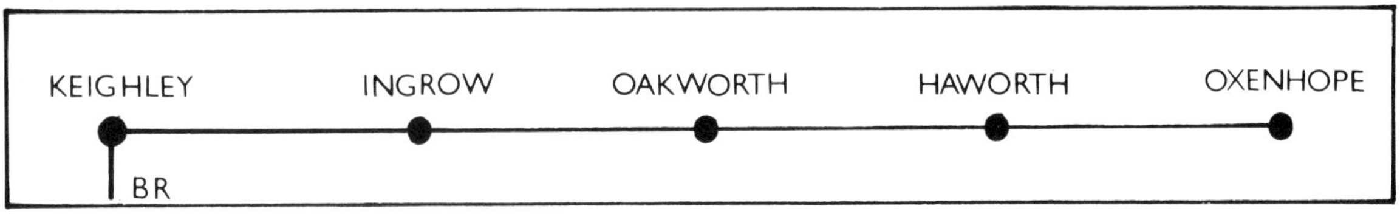

Headquarters: Haworth station, Keighley, West Yorkshire, BD22 8NJ
Telephone: Haworth 43629 (talking timetable) Haworth 45214 (other calls)
Main stations: Haworth, Oxenhope, Keighley
Other public stations: Oxenhope, Ingrow, Damens, Oakworth, Keighley
Car parks: Oxenhope, Haworth, Oakworth and Ingrow; also in Keighley and Haworth
Access by public transport: A large number of bus routes serve the area including National coach routes Nos 281/2/5/9, 291, 307/8, 318, West Yorkshire bus routes Nos 665, 765, and 760. BR services to Keighley

Above: ***Winner of the* Railway World/*Travel Britain Best Preserved Station award for 1979 was Oakworth station on the Keighley & Worth Valley Railway.*** *J. Scrace*

Locomotives

Name	*No*	*Origin*	*Class*	*Type*	*Built*
—	42765	LMS	5PF	2-6-0	1927
—	41241	LMS	2MT	2-6-2T	1949
—	45212	LMS	5MT	4-6-0	1935
—	8431	LMS	8F	2-8-0	1944
—	47279	LMS	3F	0-6-0T	1925
City of Wells	34092	SR	WC	4-6-2	1949
—	80002	BR	4MT	2-6-4T	1952
—	75078	BR	4MT	4-6-0	1956
—	78022	BR	2MT	2-6-0	1953
—	72	SR	USA	0-6-0T	1943
—	L89	GWR	5700	0-6-0PT	1929
—	52044	L&Y	2F	0-6-0	1887
—	19	L&Y	Pug	0-4-0ST	1910
—	51218	L&Y	Pug	0-4-0ST	1901
—	752	L&Y	—	0-6-0ST	1881
—	85	TVR	02	0-6-2T	1899
—	5820	USA TC	Tr203	2-8-0	1945
—	1931	SJ	WD	2-8-0	1945

Refreshment facilities: Buffet at Keighley; buffet car on some trains.
Souvenir shops: Haworth, Oxenhope, Keighley
Museums: Oxenhope (open when trains run); Haworth open daily (except Christmas).
Depots: Oxenhope, Haworth, Ingrow
Passenger trains: Steam-hauled services from Oxenhope-Keighley (5 miles). Some off-peak and local shoppers' services worked by diesel railbus.
Period of public operation: Winter (diesel) service November-March. Steam/diesel service weekends March-October. Daily during July/August. Spring Bank Holiday week and Christmas-New Year Holiday week. Please note steam services Sundays Oxenhope-Haworth November; January and February. Winter steam December (Santa Sundays) Oakworth-Oxenhope.

Industrial locomotives

Name	*No*	*Builder*	*Type*	*Built*
Fred	—	RSH (7289)	0-6-0ST	1945
—	57	RSH (7668)	0-6-0ST	1950
—	62	RSH (7673)	0-6-0ST	1950
—	63	RSH (7761)	0-6-0ST	1954
—	2226	Barclay (2226)	0-4-0ST	1946
Bellerophon	—	Haydock Foundry	0-6-0WT	1874
Sir Berkeley	—	M/Wardle (1210)	0-6-0ST	1890
Lord Mayor	—	H/Clarke (402)	0-4-0ST	1893
Hamburg	31	H/Clarke (697)	0-6-0T	1903
—	67	H/Clarke (1397)	0-6-0T	1919
Brussells	118	H/Clarke (1782)	0-6-0ST	1915
—	68077	Barclay (2215)	0-6-0ST	1947
Austins No1	—	Peckett (5003)	0-4-0D	1961
—	MDHB No 32	Hunslet (2699)	0-6-0D	1944
—	D0226	E/Electric (2345)	0-6-0D	1956
—	ESC32	H/Clarke (D816)	0-4-0D	1954
—	D2511	H/Clarke	0-6-0D	1961

Stock
2 ex-BR German-built Waggon und Maschinenbau diesel railbuses
29 coaches including examples of pre-Grouping types, BR Mk1 stock and a Pullman car

Owners
19 (L&Y Saddletanks)
51218 (L&Y Saddletanks)
43924 (the Midland 4F Preservation Society)
75078 (the Standard 4 Preservation Society)
78022 (the Standard 4 Preservation Society)

Below: ***BR Class '4MT' No 80002 at Keighley, taking water prior to departure for Oxenhope.*** *I. G. Holt*

North Yorkshire Moors Railway

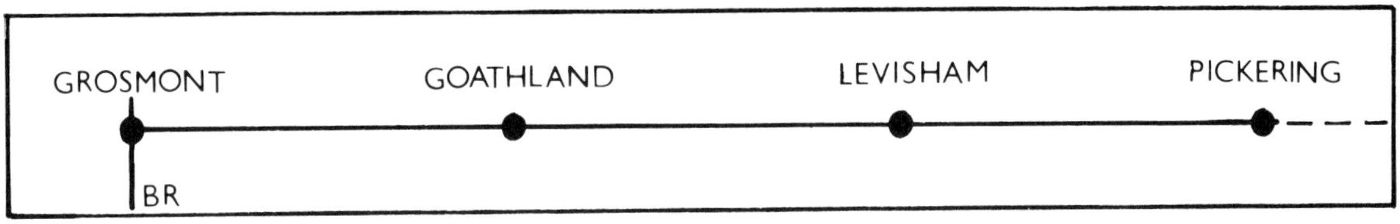

Headquarters: Pickering station, Pickering, North Yorkshire
Telephone: Pickering (0751) 72508 or 73535
Main station: Pickering
Other public stations: Grosmont, Goathland, Levisham
Car parks: Grosmont, Goathland, Levisham
Access by public transport: BR service to Grosmont or Malton. United bus services Malton-Pickering, York or Scarborough-Pickering and Whitby-Goathland and Pickering
Refreshment facilities: Available on most trains
Souvenir shops: Pickering, Goathland, Grosmont
Museum: Situated within gallery of locomotive depot at Grosmont
Depot: Grosmont
Passenger trains: Diesel and steam-hauled services Grosmont-Goathland and Pickering (full length 18 miles). Mainly steam during peak holiday season
Period of public operation: Daily Easter-October, with reduced services in early and late season
Special notes: Operates through North York Moors National Park. Information office at Pickering station. National Park Scenic service operates with diesel railcars

***Above:* Raven 0-8-0 No 2238 of 1918 heads a six coach train down to Pickering from Grosmont.** *David Eatwell*

Locomotives

Name	*No*	*Origin*	*Class*	*Type*	*Built*
—	80135	BR	4MT	2-6-4T	1956
—	13809	S&DJR	7F	2-8-0	1925
Eric Treacy	5428	LMS	5MT	4-6-0	1937
George Stephenson	4767	LMS	5MT	4-6-0	1947
—	1247	GNR	J52	0-6-0ST	1899
—	2238	NER	T2	0-8-0	1918
—	2392	NER	P3	0-6-0	1923
—	2005	LNER	K1	2-6-0	1949
—	6619	GWR	5600	0-6-2T	1928
Greene King	841	SR	S15	4-6-0	1936
—	63460	NER	T3	0-8-0	1919
—	D2207	BR/Drewry	03	0-6-0D	1953
—	D5032	BR/Sulzer	24	Bo-Bo	1959
—	D5500	BR/Brush	31	A1A-A1A	1957
*Onslaught**	D832	BR	42	B-B	1961
*Western Prince**	D1041	BR	52	C-C	1962
Western Lady	D1048	BR	52	C-C	1962
—	W79978	AC Cars	—	diesel railbus	1959

Also 2 Gloucester RC&W Co 2-car dmus
*Expected to arrive during 1980 season.

Industrial locomotives

Name	*No*	*Builder*	*Type*	*Built*
Mirvale	1	H/Clarke (1882)	0-4-0ST	1955
Meteor	31	RSH (7609)	0-6-0T	1950
Moorbarrow	47	RSH (7849)	0-6-0ST	1955
Salmon	2	Barclay (2139)	0-6-0ST	1942
—	3	Borrows (37)	0-4-0WT	1898
Teesside No 5	—	Sentinel (9629)	4wVB	1957
—	29	Lambton Rly	0-6-2T	1904
—	5	Lambton Rly	0-6-2T	1909
Stanton No 44	—	Yorkshire (2622)	0-4-0D	1956
Fowler No 21	—	Fowler (4210094)	0-4-0D	1954

Stock
Some 31 coaches including BR Mk1 stock, MET-CAM 1960 Pullmans, and LNER vehicles.
A number of freight vehicles are retained for departmental use.

Owners
841 (Essex Locomotive Society)
D5500 (on loan from the National Railway Museum)
1247 (Captain W. G. Smith)
2005 (the North Eastern Locomotive Preservation Group)
2238 (the North Eastern Locomotive Preservation Group)
13809 (the 13809 Preservation Group)
63460 (on loan from the National Railway Museum)

Middleton Railway

Headquarters: Middleton Railway Trust Ltd, Garnet Road, Leeds LS11 5TJ
Telephone: (0532) 645 424
Main station: Tunstall Road platform off Moor Road
Car parks: Tunstall Road/Moor Road (free)
Access by public transport: Bus routes Nos 74 and 76 from Leeds City station
Refreshment facilities: Tunstall Road
Souvenir shop: Tunstall Road
Museum: Collection of locomotives in Clayton's Yard which also serves as a depot
Passenger trains: Steam hauled services over a 1 mile section of line
Period of public operation: Weekends and Bank Holidays 14.00-17.00
Special notes: This is a preserved section of the country's oldest industrial railway, believed to date from 1758. Visitors ride in open goods wagons

Industrial locomotives

Name	*No*	*Builder*	*Type*	*Built*
—	2003	Peckett	0-4-0ST	1941
Henry de Lacy II	—	H/Clarke (1309)	0-4-0ST	1917
Windle	—	Borrows (53)	0-4-0WT	1909
Matthew Murray	—	Bagnall (2702)	0-4-0ST	1943
—	No 6	H/Leslie (3860)	0-4-0ST	1935
Carroll	—	H/Clarke (D631)	0-4-0D	1946
—	54	Sentinel (8839)	4wVB	1933
John Alcock	—	Hunslet (1697)	0-6-0D	1932
Courage	—	Hudson	4wD	1935

Stock
Various goods vehicles

Below: ***Ex-LNER 4wVB locomotive No 54 at Middleton.*** *H. Fisher*

Grosmont shed yard on the North Yorkshire Moors Railway with GNR No 1247 and NER No 2238 being prepared for service. In the background the 'K1' 2-6-0 leaves Grosmont Tunnel. *J. H. Cooper-Smith.*

National Railway Museum

Location: National Railway Museum, Leeman Road, York YO1 4XJ
Operating society/organisation: Science Museum, London
Telephone: York 21261 (STD Code 0904)
Car park: Limited parking for cars and coaches at the Museum
Access by public transport: The Museum is within a few minutes' walking distance of the railway and bus stations in York. The City Bus Service operates to the door
On site facilities: Souvenir shop and refreshments
Public opening: Daily, weekdays 10.00-18.00. Sundays 14.30-18.00. Closed on some public holidays
Special notes: York is a centre for 'Steam on BR' steam-hauled railtours over BR main lines. In addition to occasional charter tours, regular steam-hauled excursions operate from York during the summer season. The Museum's collection is an extensive one, and there are three or four times as many items as can be exhibited in the Museum at one time. Various items are loaned to other museums and preservation societies, while others are 'rotated' between the Museum and the reserve collection in the annexe. Within the currency of *Railways Restored 1980*, therefore, it is not possible to indicate exactly which locomotives, carriages and wagons will be on display in the Museum, but Table 1 indicates those items which form the first choice for public exhibition. For completeness the other items expected to be located at York are given in Table 2, but it is unlikely that any of these will be on public display in the immediate future

Right: Agenoria, *the oldest exhibit in the Museum built in 1829 by Foster, Rastrick & Co of Stourbridge, West Midlands for the Kingswinford Railway.*
National Railway Museum

TABLE 1
Locomotives

Name	No	Origin	Builder	Class	Type	Built
Agenoria	—	Shutt End Rly	Foster, Raistrick	—	0-4-0	1829
Columbine	—	Grand Junc Rly	—	—	2-2-2	1845
Coppernob	3	Furness Rly	Bury, Curtis & Kennedy	—	0-4-0	1846
Aerolite	66	NER	—		2-2-4T	1869
—	1	GNR	—		4-2-2	1870
—	910	NER	—		2-4-0	1875
*Chaloner**	—	—	de Winton	—	0-4-0VBT	1877
Boxhill	82	LBSCR	—	A1	0-6-0T	1880
Gladstone	214	LBSCR	—		0-4-2	1882
Wren†	—	LYR	B/Peacock (2825)	—	0-4-0ST	1887
Hardwicke	790	LNWR	—		2-4-0	1892
—	1621	NER	—	M	4-4-0	1893
—	563	LSWR	—	T3	4-4-0	1893
Gazelle	1	S&MR	Dodman	—	0-4-2WT	1893
—	490	GER	—	T26	2-4-0	1894
—	75S	Waterloo & City	—		4wE	1898
Henry Oakley	990	GNR	—		4-4-2	1898
—	737	SECR	—	D	4-4-0	1901
—	251	GNR	—		4-4-2	1902
—	1000	MR	—		4-4-0	1902
—	87	GER	—	P57	0-6-0T	1904
—	1008	LYR	—		2-4-2T	1899
—	120	LSWR	—	T9	4-4-0	1899
—	1	NER	—	—	Electric Bo-Bo	1904
—	2818	GWR	—	2800	2-8-0	1905
—	7401	LMS	—		0-6-0DM	1932
Green Arrow	4771	LNER	—	V2	2-6-2	1936
Mallard	4468	LNER	—	A4	4-6-2	1938
Duchess of Hamilton	6229	LMS	—	'Coronation'	4-6-2	1938
Ellerman Lines‡	35029	SR	—	MN	4-6-2	1948
Evening Star	92220	BR	—	9F	2-10-0	1960
—	03.090	BR	—	03	0-6-0DM	1960
—	K1*	Tasmanian Rly	B/Peacock	—	0-4-0+0-4-0T	1909
—	2392	NER	—	P3	0-6-0	1923
—	2700	LMS	—	5MT	2-6-0	1926
—	26020	BR	—	76	Electric Bo-Bo	1951
—	E5001	BR	—	71	Electric Bo-Bo	1958
—	D2860	BR	—	02	0-4-0DH	1960
Western Fusilier	1023	BR	—	'Western'	C-C	1963
—	14	—	Armstrong Whitworth (21)	—	0-4-0DE	1933
—	84.001	BR	—	84	Electric Bo-Bo	1960

TABLE 2
Locomotives

Name	No	Origin	Builder	Class	Type	Built
—	245	LSWR	—	M7	0-4-4T	1897
Cheltenham	925	SR	—	V	4-4-0	1934
*	—		R/Hornsby	—	4wD	1937
Eustace Forth	15	—	RSH(7063)	—	0-4-0ST	1942
Imperial	1	—	A/Barclay (2372)	—	0-4-0F	1956
Peveril	6	—	B/Peacock (1524)	—	2-4-0T	1875

* 2ft gauge, † 1ft 6in gauge, ‡ sectioned

Ex-L&YR 0-6-0 No 52044 shunting Oakworth yard, Keighley and Worth Valley Railway, in March 1976. *R. S. Greenwood*

Preserved Gresley Pacifics Nos 4472 **Flying Scotsman** *and 4498* **Sir Nigel Gresley** *being prepared for a main line steam tour, at Steamtown, Carnforth.* J. H. Cooper-Smith

Stock

The museum also possesses a large collection of carriages and wagons, including many pre-Grouping vehicles, Royal saloons, etc. It has an extensive display of small exhibits, nameplates, documents, etc. Items on loan from private individuals and groups are displayed in the museum from time to time.

Owners

Chaloner (on loan from Leighton Buzzard Narrow Gauge Railway)
K1 (on loan from Festiniog Railway)
6229 (on loan from Butlins Ltd)

Above: ***A general view of locomotives centred around one of the two turntables in the National Railway Museum.*** *F. Wilde*

Left: ***Some of the electric traction exhibits specially arranged for the Centenary of Electric railways in 1979.***

North Road Museum, Darlington

Location: North Road station, Darlington, County Durham
Telephone: 0325 60532
Car park: At museum site
Access by public transport: BR services to Darlington North Road station. Also good local bus service
On site facilities: Souvenir shop. Light refreshments available
Public opening: Monday-Saturday from 10.00. Sunday afternoons in summer
Special notes: The oldest railway station in the world which is still in use

Locomotives

Name	*No*	*Origin*	*Class*	*Type*	*Built*
Locomotion	1	S&DR	—	0-4-0	1825
Derwent	25	S&DR	—	0-6-0	1845
—	1275	NER	—	0-6-0	1874
—	1463	NER	—	2-4-0	1885

Industrial locomotives

Name	*No*	*Builder*	*Type*	*Built*
Met	—	H/Leslie (2800)	0-4-0ST	1909
—	—	Head Wrightson	0-4-0VB	1873

Stock
1 Stockton & Darlington Rly passenger coach

Beamish

Location: North of England Open Air Museum, near Stanley, County Durham
Telephone: Stanley (0207) 31811
Car park: At museum site
Access by public transport: Bus service No 702 from Marlborough Crescent, Newcastle upon Tyne; Bus service No 775 from Market Place, Chester-le-Street
On site facilities: 200 acre open air museum showing the past way of life of the people of the North East. Home Farm, Colliery with furnished pit cottages, Railway area with station, signal box and goods shed. Transport collection. Tram and steam loco rides. Tea Room and Victorian pub (summer only)
Public opening: Summer: May through August, every day 10.00-18.00. April and September, closed Mondays, except Bank Holidays, 10.00-18.00. Winter: October through March, 10.00-17.00, closed Mondays. Last admission is always one hour before closing time

Locomotives

Name	*No*	*Origin*	*Class*	*Type*	*Built*
—	876	NER	C	0-6-0	1889
Locomotion	1*	—	—	0-4-0	1975

*Replica

Industrial Locomotives

Name	*No*	*Builder*	*Type*	*Built*
—	41	Kitson (2509)	0-6-0PT	1883
Twizell	3	Stephenson (2730)	0-6-0T	1891
—	14	H/Leslie (3056)	0-4-0ST	1914
South Durham Malleable No 5	—	Stockton Ironworks	0-4-0ST	1900
—	—	Head Wrightson	0-4-0VB	1871
—	18	Lewin	0-4-0ST	1863
—	E1	Stephenson (2854)	2-4-0CT	1898
—	—	G. Stephenson	0-4-0	1822
—	88DS	R/Hornsby (476140)	0-4-0	1822
—	—	Simplex	0-4-0WD	1919

Right: ***The replica of*** **Locomotion** ***in steam at the North of England Museum.*** *Ian S. Carr*

On the Isle of Man Railways, 2-4-0T No 13 Kissack heads the 10.15 Douglas-Port Erin between Santon and Ballasalla. A. Bell

Yorkshire Dales Railway

Location: Embsay station, Embsay, Skipton, Yorkshire
Operating society/organisation: Yorkshire Dales Railway Museum Trust
Telephone: Skipton 4727
Car park: Embsay
Access by public transport: West Yorkshire bus routes Nos 75 or 76 from Skipton
On site facilities: Souvenir shop — specialising in transport and industrial archaeological titles, plus model railway supplies, buffet, small museum
Public opening: Every weekend, and Bank Holidays. Locomotives in steam on Sundays, Easter to end of September plus Bank Holidays
Special notes: Vintage vehicle rally mid May. Steam rides are on a short length of track, to be extended in stages to Bolton Abbey ($3\frac{1}{2}$ miles). Old Midland Rly buildings, vintage 1896 saloon, fine collection of industrial locomotives

Locomotives

No	*Origin*	*Class*	*Type*	*Built*
48151	LMS	8F	2-8-0	1942

Industrial locomotives

Name	*No*	*Builder*	*Type*	*Built*
Dorothy	—	H/Clarke (1450)	0-6-0ST	1922
Slough Estates No 5	—	H/Clarke (1709)	0-6-0ST	1939
Primrose No 2	—	Hunslet (3715)	0-6-0ST	1951
Foleshill	—	Peckett (2085)	0-4-0ST	1948
Ann	—	Sentinel (7232)	4wVB	1927
Beatrice	S119	Hunslet (2765)	0-6-0ST	1945
Airedale	—	Hunslet (1440)	0-6-0ST	1923
City Link	—	Yorkshire (2474)	0-4-0ST	1949
—	140	H/Clarke (1821)	0-6-0ST	1948
Spitfire	S112	Hunslet (2414)	0-6-0ST	1941
—	69	Hunslet (3785)	0-6-0ST	1953
—	22	Barclay (2320)	0-4-0ST	1952
BEA No 2	—	RSH (7661)	0-4-0ST	1950
—	—	Fowler (410003)	0-4-0DM	1946
Darfield No 1	—	Hunslet (3783)	0-6-0ST	1953
—	MDE15	Baguley/Drewry (2136)	4wDM	1938
—	887	Ruston Hornsby (394009)	4wDM	1955
—	—	Wickham (7610)	2w-2PMR	1957
—	—	Lister (9993)*	4wPM	1938
—	—	Lister (10225)*	4wPM	1938
King Tut†	—	Smith (—)	2-4-2	1932

* 2ft gauge
† $9\frac{1}{2}$in gauge

Stock
NER director's saloon coach
1 ex-BR suburban coach
Several freight vehicles

Bowes Railway

Location: Bowes Railway, Springwell Village, near Gateshead. (on B1288 at OS Grid Ref NZ 285589)
Operating society/organisation: Tyne & Wear Industrial Monuments Trust
Telephone: Washington 461847/816144
Car park: At museum site
Access by public transport: Northern Buses services Nos 188 Newcastle/Sunderland and 189 Newcastle/Washington
On site facilities: Shop, refreshments and guided tours of workshops. Steam hauled brake van rides. Rope haulage demonstration trains. (Operational days only)
Public opening: Static: most weekends from 10.30
Operational: Summer Bank Holiday Sundays and Mondays, and first Sunday July-October 12.00-17.30. Admission free (pay for rides)

Industrial locomotives

Name	*No*	*Builder*	*Type*	*Built*
—	22	Barclay (2274)	0-4-0ST	1949
—	101	Planet (3922)	134hp diesel	1959

Stock
21 Ordinary 10 ton wooden hopper wagons (P. J. R/Bowes, Springwell built)
16 other 10 ton wooden hopper wagons (of various pedigrees)
1 reel bogie (for rope replacement)
1 drift bogie (for shunting by rope)
1 loco coal wagon
3 materials wagons

Stationary haulage
Met-Vick/Wild, 300bhp (Blackham's Hill) 1950
BTH/Robey, 500bhp (Black Fell) 1950
Clarke Chapman, 22hp (Yard)
14ft Diam, Gravity Dilly Wheel (Springwell)

Special notes: Preserved section of the Pontop and Jarrow Railway; designed G. Stephenson; opened 1826; Only standard gauge rope-hauled incline railway in preservation; Railway's own historic workshops preserved

SCOTLAND

Strathspey Railway

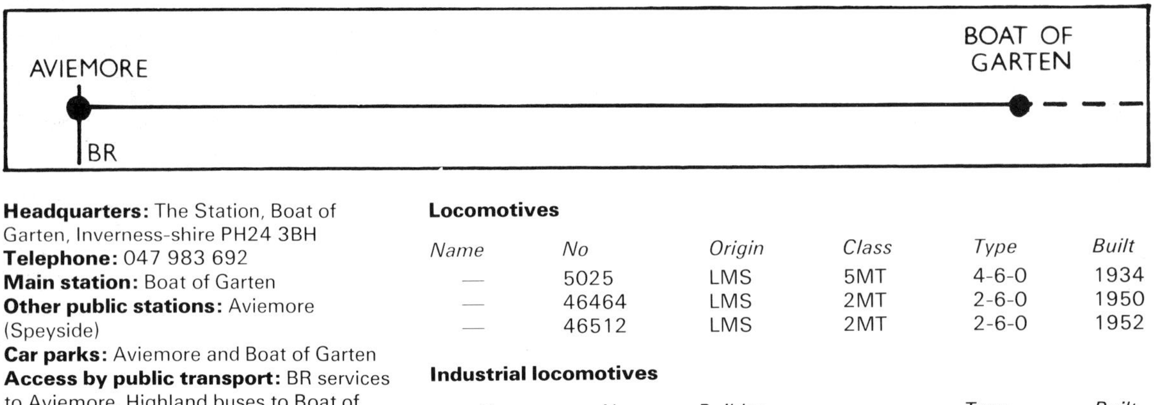

Headquarters: The Station, Boat of Garten, Inverness-shire PH24 3BH
Telephone: 047 983 692
Main station: Boat of Garten
Other public stations: Aviemore (Speyside)
Car parks: Aviemore and Boat of Garten
Access by public transport: BR services to Aviemore. Highland buses to Boat of Garten
Refreshment facilities: On train buffet car
Souvenir shop: Boat of Garten
Museum: Boat of Garten
Depot: Aviemore (not generally open to public)
Passenger trains: Steam-hauled services. Boat of Garten-Aviemore (5 miles)
Period of public operation: Weekends from mid May-September. Daily except Mondays and Fridays during July-August
Special notes: First and third class travel available on most trains. Family fares available for third class travel. Special rates/arrangements for parties

Above: ***Aviemore with Stanier Class '5' No 5025 on a train to Boat of Garten.***
R. E. Ruffell

Locomotives

Name	*No*	*Origin*	*Class*	*Type*	*Built*
—	5025	LMS	5MT	4-6-0	1934
—	46464	LMS	2MT	2-6-0	1950
—	46512	LMS	2MT	2-6-0	1952

Industrial locomotives

Name	*No*	*Builder*	*Type*	*Built*
—	48	Hunslet (2864)	0-6-0ST	1943
Cairngorm	9	RSH (7097	0-6-0ST	1943
—	60	Hunslet (3686)	0-6-0ST	1948
Forth	10	Barclay (1890)	0-4-0ST	1926
Dalurine	1	Barclay (2073)	0-4-0ST	1939
Balmenach	2	Barclay (2020)	0-4-0ST	1936
—	7	Barclay (201u)	0-6-0T	1935
Clyde	3	Barclay (2315)	0-4-0ST	1951
Inverkeith	13	H/Clarke (D613)	0-4-0D	1939
Inveresk	14	R/Hornsby (260756)	0-4-0D	1950
Madelene	39	R/Hornsby (304471)	0-4-0D	1951
Inverdon	15	Simplex (57y3)	4wDH	1957
—	—	North British (27549)	0-4-0DM	1951
Niddrie	6	Barclay (1833)	0-6-0ST	1924

Owners

46512 (the Highland Railway Co)
46464 (Dundee City Museum)

Lochty Railway

Headquarters: Balbuthie, Kilconquhar, Fife
Telephone: St Monace 210
Main station: Lochty
Car park: Lochty
Access by public transport: Nearest bus service; St Andrews-Anstruther service ($1\frac{3}{4}$ mile walk)
Souvenir shop: Lochty
Passenger trains: Steam-hauled from Lochty through the estate of J. B. Cameron ($1\frac{1}{2}$ miles)
Period of public operation: Operates only on Sundays from 14.00. Mid-June till 1st Sunday in September
Special notes: This, Britain's shortest standard gauge railway, operates entirely through the property of J. B. Cameron and no statutory authority was required in order to permit commencement of services in 1967

Locomotive

Name	*No*	*Origin*	*Class*	*Type*	*Built*
Union of South Africa	60009	LNER	A4	4-6-2	1937

Industrial locomotives

Name	*No*	*Builder*	*Type*	*Built*
—	1	Peckett (1376)	0-4-0ST	1915
—	16	Bagnall (2759)	0-6-0ST	1944
—	—	R/Hornsby (421415)	4wDM	1958

Note:
No 60009 *Union of South Africa* is stored at Markinch station for main line use on railtours.

Stock
1 ex-BR Mk 1 coach
1 LNER observation coach
1 ex-NBR 8ton box van (built 1901)
8 assorted private owner wagons

Below: ***Scotland's most frequent performer on mainline steam excursions is 'A4' 4-6-2 No 60009*** **Union Of South Africa** ***owned by John Cameron.*** *R. Payne*

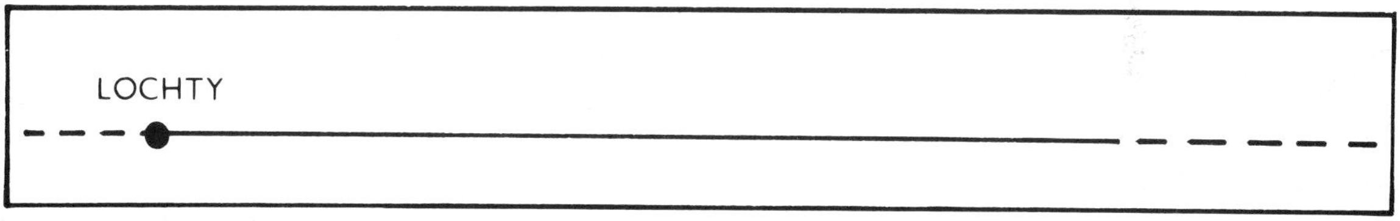

Scottish Railway Preservation Society

Location: Scottish Railway Preservation Society, Springfield Yard, off Wallace Street, Falkirk
Operating society/organisation: Scottish Railway Preservation Society
Telephone: Falkirk 20790
Car park: At the site
On site facilities: Souvenir shop and refreshments
Public opening: Static displays at weekends. Locomotives in steam Easter and August Bank Holidays and occasional weekends, 11.00-16.00
Special notes: The society promotes a number of railtours originating in the Scottish Region of BR

Locomotives

Name	*No*	*Origin*	*Class*	*Type*	*Built*
—	80105	BR	4MT	2-6-4T	1955
Morayshire	246	LNER	D49	4-4-0	1928
—	419	CR	—	0-4-4T	1907
Maude	673	NBR	—	0-6-0	1891

Industrial locomotives

Name	*No*	*Builder*	*Type*	*Built*
Lord Roberts	1	Neilson-Reid (5710)	0-6-0T	1902
Kelton Fell	13	Neilson (2203)	0-4-0ST	1876
Ellesmere	—	Haworth (Leith) (224)	0-4-0WT	1861
—	20	Barclay (2068)	0-6-0T	1939
—	3	Barclay (1937)	0-4-0ST	1928
Borrowstounness	—	Barclay (840)	0-4-0T	1899
—	—	Barclay (343)	0-6-0D	1941
City of Aberdeen	—	B/Hawthorn (912)	0-4-0ST	1887
—	47	Barclay (2157)	0-4-0ST	1943
Rotterdam	3	R/Hornsby (423658)	0-4-0D	1958

Above: ***Beautifully restored Caledonian Railway 0-4-4T No 419 with appropriate coaching stock at the SRPS Falkirk steam centre.***

Stock
Also some 20 coaches, many of which were built by pre-Grouping Scottish railway companies, and an appropriate collection of early freight vehicles

Glasgow Museum of Transport

Location: Albert Drive, Glasgow
Operating society/organisation: Glasgow Museum of Transport, 25 Albert Drive, Glasgow G41 2PE
Telephone: 041-423-8000
Car park: At museum site
Access by public transport: Pollokshields East station GGPTE bus service No 59 and others
On site facilities: Souvenir shop and tea room
Public opening: Weekdays 10.00-17.00, Sundays 14.00-17.00
Special notes: Admission free

Locomotives

Name	*No*	*Origin*	*Class*	*Type*	*Built*
—	123	CR	—	4-2-2	1866
—	828	CR	—	0-6-0	1899
—	9	G&SWR	—	0-6-0T	1917
—	103	HR	—	4-6-0	1894
Glen Douglas	256	NBR	—	4-4-0	1913
Gordon Highlander	49	GNSR	—	4-4-0	1920

Industrial locomotive

Name	*No*	*Builder*	*Type*	*Built*
—	1	Barclay (1571)	0-6-0F	1917

Stock
2 Glasgow Corporation subway cars

Owner:
828 (the Scottish Locomotive Preservation Trust)

Below: ***Ex-Highland Railway 'Jones Goods' 4-6-0 No 103 in Glasgow Museum.***
Ian Allan Library

Shanes Castle Railway

Headquarters: Antrim station, Shanes Castle Estate, Co Antrim, Northern Ireland
Telephone: Antrim 3380/2216
Main station: Antrim (SCR)
Car parks: Shanes Castle Estate, Antrim
Access by public transport: By Ulsterbus from several centres. By NI Railways to Antrim station
Refreshment facilities: Shanes Castle
Souvenir shop: Shanes Castle
Passenger trains: Steam-hauled trains from Antrim station (1½ miles) through the Shanes Castle estate. Narrow (3ft) gauge railway
Period of public operation: Sundays, April-September. Also Bank Holidays, Saturdays, June-August and Wednesdays, July-August
Special notes: Railway serves visitors to the Shanes Castle estate of Lord O'Neill which includes an extensive nature reserve

Locomotives

Name	*No*	*Builder*	*Type*	*Built*
Tyrone	1	Peckett (1026)	0-4-0T	1904
Shane	3	Barclay (2265)	0-4-0WT	1949
Nancy	—	Avonside (1547)	0-6-0T	1908
Rory	—	Simplex (11039)	0-4-0DM	1956
Nippy	—	Planet (2014)	0-4-0DM	1936

Stock
12 4-wheel carriages
3 4-wheel Tram cars

In storage
Nasmyth Wilson (830) 2-6-4T *Columbkille* 1907
Railcar No 12 Walker Bros (1934)
Railcar No 18 GNR(I) (1940)
Carriage No 14 Oldburg
Red Wagon
(Property of Dr R. Cox of the North West of Ireland Railway Society)
Ex-Co Donegal Rly

Below: ***A delightful scene on the Shanes Castle narrow gauge railway featuring Shane*** *D. Barzilay*

Isle of Man Railway

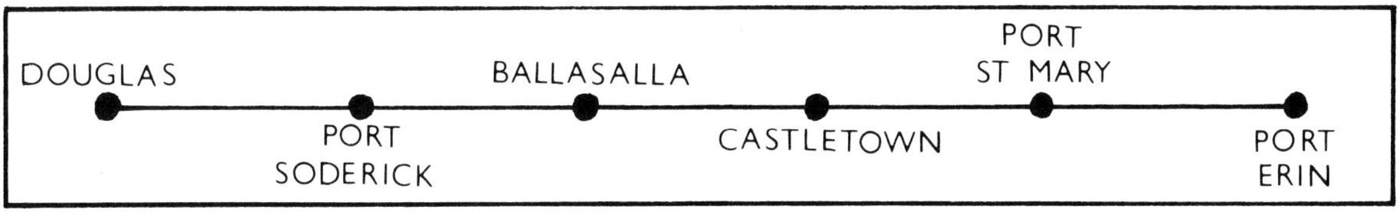

Headquarters: Isle of Man Railways, Terminus Building, Strathallan Crescent, Douglas, Isle of Man
Telephone: Douglas 4549
Main station: Douglas
Other public stations: Port Soderick, Castletown, Port Erin, Ballasalla, Port St Mary
Car parks: Douglas, Ballasalla, Castletown, Port Erin
Access by public transport: Isle of Man Transport buses to main centres
Refreshment facilities: Port Erin, Castletown
Souvenir shops: Douglas, Port Erin, Castletown
Museum: Port Erin
Depot: Douglas
Passenger trains: 3ft gauge line Douglas-Port Erin (15$\frac{1}{4}$ miles)
Period of public operation: Sundays to Fridays mid-May to mid-September
Special notes: No service operates on Saturdays

Locomotives

Name	*No*	*Builder*	*Type*	*Built*
Loch	4*	B/Peacock (1416)	2-4-0T	1874
Mona	5	B/Peacock (1417)	2-4-0T	1874
Douglas	9	B/Peacock (3815)	2-4-0T	1896
G. H. Wood	10	B/Peacock (4462)	2-4-0T	1905
Maitland	11*	B/Peacock (4463)	2-4-0T	1905
Hutchinson	12*	B/Peacock (5162)	2-4-0T	1908
Kissack	13*	B/Peacock (5382)	2-4-0T	1910
—	19*	—	diesel railcar	1950
—	20*	—	diesel railcar	1951

*Operational, the remainder are stored out of use not on display.

Stored in museum at Port Erin

Name	*No*	*Builder*	*Type*	*Built*
Sutherland	1	B/Peacock (1253)	2-4-0T	1873
Caledonia	15	Dubs & Co (2178)	0-6-0T	1885
Mannin	16	B/Peacock (6296)	2-4-0T	1926

Railway Preservation Society of Ireland

Location: Whitehead Excursion station
Operating society: Railway Preservation Society of Ireland
Telephone: Whitehead (096 033) 8567
Car park: At the site
Access by public transport: Northern Ireland Railways services from Belfast (York Road) or Larne Harbour: Ulster Bus service
On site facilities: Souvenir shop open on Sundays during July and August
Public opening: Sundays during July and August
Special notes: The RPSI is noted for its main line railtours operated each year using its own rolling stock and coaches. In 1980 the annual two-day railtour will be from Dublin to Tralee via Mallow and Killarny, using Nos 171 and 186. The railtour will take place on 17/18 May 1980. Provisional dates for the Society's famous 'Portrush Flyer' public excursions are 16 July and 16 August 1980

Locomotives

Name	*No*	*Origin*	*Class*	*Type*	*Built*
Merlin	85	GNR (I)	V	4-4-0	1932
Slieve Gullion	171	GNR (I)	S	4-4-0	1913
—	4	LMS (NCC)	WT	2-6-4T	1947
—	184*	GS&WR	J15	0-6-0	1880
—	186*	GS&WR	J15	0-6-0	1879
—	461*	D&SER	K2	2-6-0	1922
Lough Erne	—*	SL&NCR	—	0-6-4T	1949

Industrial locomotives

Name	*No*	*Builder*	*Type*	*Built*
Guinness	3	H/Clarke (1152)	0-4-0ST	1919
R. H. Smyth	3	Avonside (2021)	0-6-0ST	1928
—	23	Planet	0-4-0D	—

Stock
The Society also owns some 20 coaches, normally resident at Whitehead, where a small number of freight wagons are also preserved

*Normally based in the Republic of Ireland

Association of Railway Preservation Societies Ltd

Company Limited by Guarantee and not having a share capital.
Registered in England No 1222717

(Registered Office: 21 Market Place, Wednesbury, West Midlands WS10 7AY)

Directors/Council of Management

Chairman
Captain Peter F. Manisty, RN (Retd), 2 Cleaver Square, Kennington, London SE11 4DW. Tel: 01-735 5012 (Ansafone fitted)

Vice-Chairman
Mr M. D. Crew, BSc, 34 Templegate Road, Whitkirk, Leeds, Yorks LS15 0HE. Tel: 0532-648939

Company Secretary and Treasurer
Mr R. T. Yates, FCA, 21 Market Place, Wednesbury, West Midlands WS10 7AY

General Secretary
Mr D. P. Madden, Sheringham station, Norfolk NR26 8RA. Tel: 0263-822045

Minutes Secretary
Mr E. V. Boxell, 17 Azalea Close, Uxbridge Road, Hanwell, London W7 3QA. Tel: 01-840 2917

Membership Secretary
Mr P. J. Brown, 52 Burniston Drive, Huddersfield, West Yorks HD3 3PP

Meetings Organiser
Mr J. C. Jeffery, 'Failte', 15 Hemmingford Crescent, Stanground, Peterborough PE2 8LL

Legal Officer and Membership Constitutions
Mr D. Morgan, 7 Cheyne Place, London SW3 4HH

Correspondence Secretary
Mr P. J. G. Ransom, 'Woodside', Craggan, Lochearnhead FK19 8QD

Publicity Officer
Mr J. E. Rumens, 31 Dornton Road, South Croydon, Surrey CR2 7DR. Tel: 01-688 2593

Press and Public Relations Officer
Mr B. T. Wright, 32 Hawthorne Avenue, Mitcham, Surrey CR4 3DN. Tel: 01-648 4924 (Ansafone fitted)

Newsletter Assistant and Secretary
Mrs S. M. Youell, 5 North Grange Mount, Leeds, Yorks LS6 2BY

Newsletter Editor
Rev E. J. Buck, 40 Chapel Lane, Wymondham, Norfolk

All general correspondence and enquiries should be addressed to the: General Secretary, ARPS, Sheringham station, Norfolk NR26 8RA, England. Tel: 0263-822045

Private Membership Application Form (1980)

To a person actively interested in nationwide railway preservation as opposed to one particular preservation scheme, PRIVATE MEMBERSHIP of the ASSOCIATION OF RAILWAY PRESERVATION SOCIETIES LTD can offer many advantages. Three major meetings are organised annually, often at the railway site of a leading Full Member Society. Here one can meet well known personalities in the railway preservation world, and the host society invariably lays on a full day's programme which is both stimulating and enjoyable.

Regular duplicated newletters are sent to members, containing mostly the latest news of member societies' activities but also full of interesting titbits such as lists of steam locomotives for sale.

To: P. J. Brown, Esq, 52 Burniston Drive, Huddersfield, West Yorks HD3 3PP

Name ....
(BLOCK LETTERS PLEASE)

Address ....

....

Post Code .... Telephone ....

Subscription enclosed .... Donation enclosed ....

Private membership costs £4 per year (1 April-31 March) payable on a sliding scale. For subscriptions taken out for the first year as follows:
Applications sent in from 1 January-31 March (£5);
1 April-30 June (£4); 1 July-30 September (£3);
1 October-31 December (£2).

Members of the Association of Railway Preservation Societies

Full Members

Bluebell Railway Preservation Society: Mr P. A. Cooper, 28 Courtlands, Haywards Road, Haywards Heath, West Sussex RH16 4JD

Brockham Museum Association/Brockham Museum Trust: Mr D. H. Smith, 14 Sydney Road, Haywards Heath, West Sussex RH16 1PZ

The Bulleid Society Limited: Mr R. T. Price, Brunswick House, 30 Wandsworth Road, London SW8 2LG

H. P. Bulmer Limited: Mr A. V. Ryder, 34 Wordsworth Road, Whitecross, Hereford HR4 0QB

Cambrian Railways Society Limited: Mr J. L. D. Price, 9 Liverpool Road West, Oswestry, Salop SY11 NZ

Chasewater Railway Society: Mr B. J. Bull, 173 Parkeston Crescent, Kingstanding, Birmingham B44 0PS

Colne Valley Railway Company Limited: Mr J. R. Hymas, Castle Hedingham station, Yeldham Road, Castle Hedingham, Halstead, Essex CO9 3DZ

Corris Railway Society: Mr A. H. Lawson, 165 Gynsill Lane, Anstey, Leicester LE7 7AN

Dart Valley Railway Association: Mr K. Northwood, Secretary, Brierley, Old Totnes Road, Buckfastleigh, Devon TQ11 0BY

Dean Forest Railway Society Limited: Mr C. A. Bladon, Laurel Cottage, Northwood Green, Westbury-on-Severn, Gloucestershire

Derwent Valley Railway Company: Mr J. Acklam, DVR Co, Layerthorpe station, York YO3 7XS

Dinting Railway Centre Limited (Bahamas Locomotive Society): Mr K. J. Tait, Secretary, 15 Priestnall Road, Heaton Mersey, Stockport SK4 3HR

Dowty Railway Preservation Society: Mr R. H. Wales, 7 Lypiatt Street, Tivoli, Cheltenham, Gloucestershire

East Lancashire Railway Preservation Society: Mr H. Hatcher, Bury Transport Museum, Castlecroft Road, Bury, Lancashire BL9 0LN

East Somerset Railway Company Limited: Mr I. Roach, General Manager, The Railway station, West Cranmore, Shepton Mallet, Somerset

Festiniog Railway Society Limited: Mr A. Shooter, Managing Director, Islinfold, Marchburn Lane, Riding Mill, Northumberland NE44 6DN

Foxfield Light Railway Society Limited: Mr B. Allen, 25 Drubbery Lane, Dresden, Stoke-on-Trent ST3 4BH

Friends of the National Railway Museum: Mr O. J. F. Whitaker, c/o The National Railway Museum, Leeman Road, York YO2 4XJ

Great Eastern Railway Group: Mr J. Watling, 22 Manor Way, Chingford, London E4 6NW

Great Western Society Limited: Mr W. J. Smith, GWS, Didcot, Oxon OX11 7NJ

Gwili Railway Company Limited: Mr R. L. Pittard, 61 Chantal Avenue, Penyfai, Bridgend, Mid-Glamorgan CF31 4NW

H Class Trust: Mr E. R. C. Oades, 5 Senlac Way, St Leonards-on-Sea, Sussex

Irish Steam Preservation Society Limited: Mrs Olive Condell, Secretary, Bay House, Main Street, Stradbally, County Laois

Isle of Man Steam Railway Supporters Association: Mr R. J. F. Clark, Secretary, 8 Richmond Close, Glen Park, Douglas, IoM

Keighley and Worth Valley Railway Preservation Society: Mr P. Eastham, Secretary, 79 Cedar Street, Skew Bridge, Blackburn, Lancs BB1 9TQ

Lakeside Railway Society (Lakeside & Haverthwaite Railway): Mr J. Houghton, 'Avonlea', Garstang Road, Catterall, Garstang, Preston PR3 0HD

Leighton Buzzard Narrow Gauge Railway Society Limited: Mr D. F. Trevelion, Secretary, 18 Hornbeam Close, Leighton Buzzard, Bedfordshire LU7 8UX

The Locomotion Trust: Mr L. Wilson, Witton House, Witton le Wear, Bishop Auckland, County Durham DL14 0AZ

Locomotive Club of Great Britain: Mr R. L. Patrick, 52 Penrhyn Road, Northampton NN4 9ED

Locomotive Owners Group (Scotland) Limited: Mr J. L. Stevenson, 22 Comely Bank Place, Edinburgh EH4 1DU

Locomotion Enterprises Limited: Mr M. G. Satow, 50 Church Lane, Ormesby, Middlesbrough, Cleveland TS7 9AU

Maid Marian Locomotive Fund: Mr D. C. Carrington, 223 Sunnybank Road, Unsworth, Bury, Lancashire BL9 8JU

Main Line Steam Trust Limited: Mr S. L. Jacobs, Great Central Railway station, Loughborough, Leicestershire LE11 1SS

Merchant Navy Locomotive Preservation Society Limited: Mr R. Abercrombie, 60 Burgoyne Road, Sunbury-on-Thames, Middlesex

Middleton Railway Trust Limited: Mr J. D. Edwards, 30 Parsonage Lane, Bishops Stortford, Hertfordshire CM23 5BG

Mid Hants Railway Preservation Society Limited: Mr C. W. Lewis, Brooklands, 12 Winston Rise, Four Marks, Alton, Hampshire GU34 5HW

Midland & Great Northern Joint Railway Society Limited: The Secretary, Sheringham station, Sheringham, Norfolk NR26 8RA

Midland 4F Preservation Society: Mr I. Johnson, 3 Meldon Avenue, Chase Park, Sherburn, Durham DH6 1JX

Midland Railway Trust Limited: Mr R. Clegg, 9 Hawthorn Crescent, Findern, Derby DE6 6AN

Norfolk Railway Society: Mr E. W. Beckett, 1 Virginia Close, Sprowston, Norwich, Norfolk NR7 8JJ

North Eastern Locomotive Preservation Group: Mr D. Hanson, 10 Crossgate, Durham

North York Moors Historical Railway Trust: Chief Executive & General Manager, Trust Office, Pickering station, Park Street, Pickering YO18 7AJ

Peterborough Railway Society Limited (Nene Valley Railway): Mr K. G. Faulkner, General Manager, Nene Valley Railway, PO Box 3, Touthill Close, City Road, Peterborough PE1 1UJ

Quainton Railway Society Limited: Mr A. Harland, 19 Poles Hill, Chesham, Bucks HP5 2QR

Railway Preservation Society of Ireland: Mr R. Morton, 2 Cranmore Park, Belfast BT9 6JG

Ravenglass and Eskdale Railway Preservation Society Limited: Mr D. Pickup, The Retreat, Ravenglass, Cumbria CA18 1SW

Scottish Railway Preservation Society: Mr I. R. Gordon, Secretary, 14 Ardbeg Avenue, High Burnside, Glasgow

Severn Valley Railway Company Limited: Mr M. J. Draper, 'Wynniatts', The Hill, Abberley, Worcester WR6 6BZ

Sittingbourne & Kemsley Light Railway Limited: Mr M. Burton, 85 Balmoral Avenue, Gillingham, Kent

Stanier 8F Locomotive Society Limited: Mr K. Robey, 60 Peake Avenue, Nuneaton, Warwickshire CV11 6DW

Steam in Hereford Limited (6000 Locomotive Association): Mr E. T. Taylor, 18 Merestone Road, Redhill, Hereford HR2 7PS

Stour Valley Railway Preservation Society: Mr L. Houghton, Secretary, Willowbrook, Warley Road, Great Warley, Brentwood, Essex

Southern Electric Group: Mr Mr A. C. Holmewood, 48 Church Lane, Chessington, Surrey KT9 2DW

Tenterden Railway Company Limited (Kent & East Sussex Railway): The Company Secretary, Tenterden Railway Company Limited, Tenterden Town station, Tenterden, Kent TN30 6HE

Tyne & Wear Industrial Monuments Trust: Sandyford House, Archbold Terrace, Newcastle-upon-Tyne NE2 1ED

Vintage Carriages Trust: Mr C. G. Smyth, 3 Mill Hey, Haworth, Keighley, West Yorkshire

Wainwright 'C' Preservation Society: Mr I. DeMaid, 69 Bromley Gardens, Bromley, Kent BR2 0ES

Welshpool and Llanfair Light Railway Preservation Company Limited: Mr J. C. Dickenson, 24 Solent Drive, Bolton, Lancs BL3 1RN

West Somerset Railway Company Limited: Mr C. M. Van Den Arend, The Railway station, Minehead, Somerset TA24 5BG

Wight Locomotive Society: Mr R. Macdonald, The Station, Havenstreet, Ryde, Isle of Wight PO33 4DS

Worcester Locomotive Society: Mr D. R. G. Nowell, 1 Ranelagh Street, Hereford

275 Railway Squadron RCT (V): Capt W. G. Goodman RCT (V), 9 Yorkwood, Liss, Hants GU33 7AF

1247 Society: Capt W. G. Smith, Flat 3, 28 Park Avenue, Bedford MK40 2LR

1708 Locomotive Preservation Trust Limited: Mr G. S. Mimms, 15 Windsor Road, Barton-le-Clay, Beds

6201 Princess Elizabeth Society Limited: Mr E. Whitlock, 7 Cherry Walk, Lydney, Glos. Tel: Lydney 8026

Associate Members

Avonside Steam Preservation Society: Mr K. Rodgers, 58 Castle Street, Cambridge CB3 0AP

A4 Locomotive Society Limited: Mr G. R. Pope, Secretary, 25 Acacia Road, St Johns Wood, London

Battle of Britain Locomotive Preservation Society: Mr T. Missen, 15 Belfast Mead, Lyneham, Chippenham, Wiltshire

Bressingham Steam Engine Trust: Mr A. Bloom, Bressingham Hall, Bressingham, Diss, Norfolk IP22 2AB

Britannia Locomotive Society: Mr R. L. Kingston, 'Lysander', Merchant Lane, Cranfield, Bedfordshire

Cadeby Light Railway: Rev E. R. Boston, Cadeby Rectory, Cadeby, Hinckley, Nuneaton, Warwickshire

Caerphilly Railway Society Limited: Mr A. Smith, 51 Worcester Crescent, Newport, Gwent

Conwy Valley Railway Museum Limited: Mr A. Pratt, Conwy Valley Railway Museum, Betws-y-Coed, Gwynedd LL24 0AL

Camelot Locomotive Society: Mr P. W. Gibbs, 71 Broadstone Road, Harpenden, Hertfordshire AL5 1RE

Forest Pannier Tank Fund: Mr J. S. Metherall, 15 Sudbrook Way, Gloucester

Forest Prairie Fund: Mr P. Skinner, 18 Waverley Road, Redland, Bristol BS6 6EX

Gravesend Railway Enthusiasts Society: Mr T. W. Hanks, 68 The Fairway, Gravesend, Kent DA11 7LW

Great Western Preservations Limited: Mr A. R. Machon, 15 Calder Close, Maidenhead, Berks SL6 7RS

Great Central Railway Coach Group: Mr J. S. Parsons, 8 Grendon Way, Bierton, Aylesbury, Bucks HP22 5DD

The Gresley Society: Mr P. Holmes, Argyll Cottage, Thurgarton Quarters, Oxton Road, Southwell, Notts NG25 0RW

GWR 813 Preservation Fund: Mr P. Goss, 23 Hatchmere, Thornbury, Bristol BS12 2EU

Hallamshire Railway Preservation Society: Mr D. Lawson, 100 Ellerton Road, Firth Park, Sheffield S5 6UG

Hexham Rolling Stock Group: Mr G. Hall, 24 Welton Close, Stocksfield, Northumberland NE43 7EP

Historic Rolling Stock Fund: Mr T. C. Bowen, 5 Bedford Road, Wallasey, Merseyside L43 5EB

Hull and Barnsley Railway Stock Fund: Mr A. Halman, Secretary, 6 Chequerfield Court, Chequerfield Avenue, Pontefract, West Yorks WF8 2TQ. Tel: 0977-73493. Mr N. Fleetwood, Publicity Officer, 36 St Pauls Road, Thornton Heath, Surrey CR4 8NB

Ivatt Locomotive Trust: Mr R. B. Miller, Ducal, 25 Loudham Road, Little Chalfont, Amersham, Buckinghamshire

Lambton No 29 Syndicate: Mr J. M. Richardson, c/o Midland Bank Limited, 1 Murray Street, Filey, North Yorkshire YO14 9DB

Lancashire & Yorkshire Saddletanks Fund: Mr R. S. Greenwood, 8 Oxford Avenue, Rochdale, Lancashire

Liverpool Locomotive Preservation Group: Mr E. Wheelwright, 6 Mill Way, Nantwich, Cheshire

Llangollen Railway Society: Mr T. A. S. Parkins, PO Box 10, Stanmore, Middlesex

Lloyds Railway Society: Mr P. E. Wood, Leslie & Godwin (UK) Ltd, Dunster House, Mark Lane, London EC3P 3AD

LM 2MT 46464 Trust: Mr I. N. Fraser, Palace Gates, Viewfield Road, Arbroath, Angus DD11 2BS

London & North Western Society: Mr J. C. James, Solaby, 4 Longview Drive, Huyton, Liverpool L36 6EE

Lord Fisher Locomotive Group: Mr B. G. Buckfield, C/o Cranmore station, West Cranmore, Shepton Mallet, Somerset

Manchester Rail Travel Society: Mr F. G. Cronin, 12 Chiltern Road, Ramsbottom, Lancashire

Manx Electric Railway Society: Mr R. J. F. Clark, ARPS Delegate, 8 Richmond Close, Glenpark, Douglas, Isle of Man

*Maunsell Locomotive Society (*incorporating *847 Locomotive Preservation Group):* Mr M. Allen, General Secretary, 51 Friar Crescent, Brighton, Sussex BN1 6NL

Maunsell 'Q' Locomotive Preservation Society: Mr D. Preece, 8 Podsmead Place, Gloucester GL1 5PD

North Eastern Railway Coach Group: Mr P. J. Brumby, 48 Laburnum Walk, Gilberdyke, Brough, Humberside HU15 2TU

North Staffordshire Railway Society: Mr I. J. Bowland, 78 Park Lane, Sandbach, Cheshire. Mr A. Hall, 13 Harris Street, Penkhull, Stoke-on-Trent, Staffs ST4 7EZ

North West of Ireland Railway Society: Mr D. J. Lloyd, 3 Knockwellan Park, Londonderry BT47 2JB

Railway Stock Restoration Group: Mr A. Goss, 60 Westonfields, Totnes, Devon

Railway Vehicle Preservations: Mr D. Pearce, 77 Gosling House, Sutton Street, Shadwell, London E1

Rheilffordd Llyn Tegid Limited (Bala Lake Railway): Mr G. H. Barnes, General Manager, 'Yr Orsaf', Llanuwchllyn, Bala, Gwynedd

Romney Hythe & Dymchurch Railway Holding Company Limited: Mr W. McAlpine, 40 Bernard Street, London WC1

Salisbury Steam Locomotive Preservation Trust: Mr E. J. Roper, 33 Victoria Road, Wilton, Salisbury, Wiltshire SP2 0OZ

Shackerstone Railway Society Limited: Mr D. F. Pratley, Secretary, 127 Loughborough Road, Whitwick, Leicestershire

Somerset & Dorset Railway Museum Trust: Mr M. Palmer, The Haven, Chandlers Lane, Edington, Bridgwater, Somerset

Southern Steam Trust: Mr M. D. Stone, Southern Steam Trust, The station, Swanage, Dorset

South Western Circle: Mr C. Chivers, 96 Canterbury Way, Stevenage, Hertfordshire SG1 4DA

Stanier Black Five Locomotive Preservation Society: Mr D. J. Porter, 4 High Street, Shoreham, Kent

Steamport Southport: Mr C. Forrest, 14 Franklands, Longton, Preston, Lancashire

Steam Power Trust '65: Mr K. H. Cockerill, 30 Hartburn Lane, Stockton-on-Tees TS18 3QH

Strathspey Railway Association: Mr R. Black, 37 Castle Avenue, Balloch, Alexandria, Dunbartonshire G83 8HU

Strathspey Railway Company Limited: Mr D. B. Barclay, 42 Forglen Cresent, Bridge of Allan, Stirlingshire FK9 4BQ

Urie S15 Preservation Group: Mr G. Styles, 29 Irwin Road, Guildford, Surrey GU2 5PW

Vale of Rheidol Railway Supports Association: Mr G. T. Jones, 5 Erw Goch, Waunfawr, Aberystwyth, Dyfed SY23 3AZ

Welsh Industrial and Maritime Museum: Dr E. S. Owen-Jones, Welsh Industrial & Maritime Museum, Bute Street, Docks, Cardiff CF1 6AN

West Somerset Steam Railway Trust Limited: Maj A. S. Griffiths, Minehead Railway station, Minehead, Somerset TA24 5BG

Winchcombe Railway Museum Association: Mr T. R. Petchey, 23 Gloucester Street, Winchcombe, Glos

847 Locomotive Preservation Group: Refer to 'Maunsell Locomotive Society'

1857 Society: Mr K. R. Bowen, 18 Lochmore Close, Hollycroft, Hinckley, Leics

6024 Preservation Society Limited: Mr W. A. Wilkinson, Secretary, 12 Tudor Square, Hayes End, Middlesex UB3 2QT

9642 Preservation Group: Mr W. T. Jones, 'Bryn Awelon', 55 Salisbury Road, Maesteg, Glamorgan CF34 9EH

45428 Stanier Class Five Locomotive Society Limited: Mr J. B. Hollingsworth, 'Creua', Llanfrothen, Penrhyndeudraeth, Gwynedd LL48 6SH

71000 Duke of Gloucester Steam Locomotive Trust Ltd: Mr M. D. Johnson, 9 Ladybank, Birch Hill, Bracknell, Berks

ARPS Affiliations

Association of Minor Railway Companies: Mr A. G. W. Garraway, Chairman, Festiniog Railway Company, Harbour station, Porthmadog, Gwynedd LL49 9NF. Mr J. Acklam, Secretary, Derwent Valley Railway Company, Layerthorpe station, York YO3 7XS

Narrow Gauge Railways of Wales Joint Marketing Panel: Mr D. Woodhouse, Wharf station, Towyn, Gwynedd LL36 9EY

Transport Trust: Mr P. R. Davis, 76 Stewarts Road, London SW8 4DE

Index

Page numbers in bold type refer to timetables

Hythe and Dungeness — Romney, Hythe & Dymchurch Railway

Spring, Autumn and Winter
Daily 29 March-3 April, 21 April-2 May, 6-23 May, 22-28 September
also Saturdays & Sundays 1-23 March, 4 October-30 November
(but between New Romney and Dungeness, only when note A applies)

		L	NX	L	NX	A	L	A	NX	A
Dungeness	d					14 40		15 40		16 40
Pilot Halt	d					*		*		*
Lade Halt	d					*		*		*
Maddieson's	d					14 55		15 55		16 55
Greatstone Halt	d					*		*		*
New Romney	a					15 10		16 10		17 10
New Romney	d	11 14	12 14	13 14	14 14		15 14		16 14	17 14
St Mary's Bay	d	11 23	12 23	13 23	14 23		15 23		16 23	17 23
Dymchurch	d	11 30	12 30	13 30	14 30		15 30		16 30	17 30
Hythe	a	11 50	12 50	13 50	14 50		15 50		16 50	17 50

		L	NX	A	L	A	NX	A	L	NX	A
Hythe	d	12 10	13 10		14 10		15 10		16 10	17 10	18 10
Dymchurch	d	12 28	13 28		14 28		15 28		16 28	17 28	18 28
St Mary's Bay	d	12 33	13 33		14 33		15 33		16 33	17 33	18 33
New Romney	a	12 45	13 45		14 45		15 45		16 45	17 45	18 45
New Romney	d			13 48		14 48		15 48			
Greatstone Halt	d			*		*		*			
Maddieson's	d			14 00		15 00		16 00			
Lade Halt	d			*		*		*			
Pilot Halt	d			*		*		*			
Dungeness	a			14 20		15 20		16 20			

Early and Late Season
Daily 4-5 April, 8-20 April, 3-5 May, 2 June-25 July, 8-21 September

		FO				B			B	B			B		
Hythe	d		10 20	11 20	12 20		13 20	14 20		14 50	15 20	16 20	16 50	17 20	18 20
Dymchurch	d		10 38	11 38	12 38		13 38	14 38		15 08	15 38	16 38	17 08	17 38	18 38
St Mary's Bay	d		10 43	11 43	12 43		13 43	14 43		15 13	15 43	16 43	17 13	17 43	18 43
New Romney	a		10 55	11 55	12 55		13 55	14 55		15 25	15 55	16 55	17 25	17 55	18 55
New Romney	d	09 15		11 58		12 58	13 58		14 58		15 58				
Greatstone Halt	d	*		*		*	*		*		*				
Maddiesons's	d	*		12 10		13 10	14 10		15 10		16 10				
Lade Halt	d	*		*		*	*		*		*				
Pilot Halt	d	*		*		*	*		*		*				
Dungeness	a	09 40		12 30		13 30	14 30		15 30		16 30				

			FO					B	B			B	B		
Dungeness	d		09 45				12 50		13 50		14 50		15 55		16 55
Pilot Halt	d		*				*		*		*		*		*
Lade Halt	d		*				*		*		*		*		*
Maddieson's	d		10 05				13 05		14 05		15 05		16 10		17 10
Greatstone Halt	d		*				*		*		*		*		*
New Romney	a		10 20				13 20		14 20		15 20		16 25		17 25
New Romney	d	09 24		10 24	11 24	12 24	13 24	13 54		14 24	15 24	15 54		16 29	17 29
St Mary's Bay	d	09 33		10 33	11 33	12 33	13 33	14 03		14 33	15 33	16 03		16 38	17 38
Dymchurch	d	09 40		10 40	11 40	12 40	13 40	14 10		14 40	15 40	16 10		16 45	17 45
Hythe	a	10 00		11 00	12 00	13 00	14 00	14 30		15 00	16 00	16 30		17 05	18 05

High Season Service Daily 6-7 April, 24 May-1 June, 26 July-7 September

		FO			SX		SX		SX	GJ SO				SX		SO	SX		SX		
Hythe	d		10 20	11 20	11 50	12 20	12 50	13 20	13 50	14 04	14 20	14 50	15 20	15 50	16 20	16 50	16 50	17 20	17 50	18 20	19 20
Dymchurch	d		10 38	11 38	12 08	12 38	13 08	13 38	14 08		14 38	15 08	15 38	16 08	16 38		17 08	17 38	18 08	18 38	19 38
St Mary's Bay	d		10 43	11 43	12 13	12 43	13 13	13 43	14 13		14 43	15 13	15 43	16 13	16 43		17 13	17 43	18 13	18 43	19 43
New Romney	a		10 55	11 55	12 25	12 55	13 25	13 55	14 25		14 55	15 25	15 55	16 25	16 55	17 15	17 25	17 55	18 25	18 55	19 55
New Romney	d	09 15	10 58	11 58		12 58		13 58			14 58		15 58		16 58						
Greatstone Halt	d	*	*	*		*		*			*		*		*						
Maddiesons's	d	*	11 10	12 10		13 10		14 10			15 10		16 10		17 10						
Lade Halt	d	*	*	*		*		*			*		*		*						
Pilot Halt	d	*	*	*		*		*			*		*		*						
Dungeness	a	09 40	11 30	12 30		13 30		14 30		14 46	15 30		16 30		17 30						

			FO		SX		SX				SX		SX		GJ SO	SX		SX		
Dungeness	d		09 45					11 50		12 50		13 50		14 50	15 35		15 50		16 55	17 55
Pilot Halt	d		*					*		*		*		*			*		*	*
Lade Halt	d		*					*		*		*		*			*		*	*
Maddieson's	d		10 05					12 05		13 05		14 05		15 05			16 05		17 10	18 10
Greatstone Halt	d		*					*		*		*		*			*		*	*
New Romney	a		10 20					12 20		13 20		14 20		15 20			16 20		17 25	18 25
New Romney	d	09 24		10 24	10 54	11 24	11 54	12 24	12 54	13 24	13 54	14 24	14 54	15 24		15 54	16 24	16 54	17 29	18 29
St Mary's Bay	d	09 33		10 33	11 03	11 33	12 03	12 33	13 03	13 33	14 03	14 33	15 03	15 33		16 03	16 33	17 03	17 38	18 38
Dymchurch	d	09 40		10 40	11 10	11 40	12 10	12 40	13 10	13 40	14 10	14 40	15 10	15 40		16 10	16 40	17 10	17 45	18 45
Hythe	a	10 00		11 00	11 30	12 00	12 30	13 00	13 30	14 00	14 30	15 00	15 30	16 00	16 17	16 30	17 00	17 30	18 05	19 05

* Stops only on request to the guard (to alight) or on giving a handsignal to the driver (to board)
A Runs only on Sundays 27 April, 11, 18 May, 28 September
B Runs on Sundays, and also runs daily 3-5 May, 23 June, 25 July
C Runs on Sundays, and also runs daily except Tuesdays 3-5 May, 23 June 25 July
F, FO Fridays only
GJ *The Golden Jubilee* Runs non-stop Hythe to Dungeness

L Sundays only, but also Saturdays in November
N, NX Does not run during November
S, SO Saturdays only
SX Daily except Saturdays
X Daily except Saturdays

Alresford and Ropley — Mid-Hants Railway
Operated by steam traction

Saturdays 22 March to 25 October
Also Friday 4 April

Alresford	d		13 30	14 20	15 10	16 00	16 50	17 55
Ropley	a		13 41	14 31	15 21	16 11	17 01	18 06
Ropley	d	13 04	13 54	14 44	15 34	16 24	17 24	
Alresford	a	13 13	14 03	14 53	15 43	16 33	17 33	

Sundays 23, 30 March, 13, 20, 27 April
11, 18 May, 7 September to 26 October

Alresford d	11 30	12 30	13 30	14 20	15 10	16 00	16 50	17 55
Ropley a	11 41	12 41	13 41	14 31	15 21	16 11	17 01	18 06
Ropley d	12 04	13 04	13 54	14 44	15 34	16 24	17 24	
Alresford a	12 13	13 13	14 03	14 53	15 43	16 33	17 33	

Sundays 6 April, 4, 25 May to 31 August
Also Bank Holiday Mondays 7 April, 5, 26 May,
25 August

Alresford	d	11 30	12 30	13 30		14 30	15 05	15 40	16 15	16 50	17 35	17 55
Ropley	a	11 41	12 41	13 41		14 41	15 16	15 51	16 26	17 01	17 46	18 06
Ropley	d	12 04	13 04	13 54	14 19	14 54	15 29	16 04	16 39	17 24		18 19
Alresford	a	12 13	13 13	14 03	14 28	15 03	15 38	16 13	16 48	17 33		18 28

Additional trains may operate as required

Train services shown here are subject to alteration or cancellation at any time without prior notice, although every effort will be made to avoid inconvenience

Car Parking: Free parking is provided at Alresford station — passengers are requested not to travel to Ropley by car as space for public parking is very limited

Sheffield Park and Horsted Keynes — Bluebell Railway
Operated by steam traction

Peak Sundays and Bank Holidays
Sundays 6 April and 25 May to 28 September inclusive
Bank Holiday Mondays 7 April, 5, 26 May and 25 August

								E		E		E		
Sheffield Park	d	10 25	11 25	12 23		13 20	13 40	14 28	14 50	15 37	15 55	16 42	17 00	17 55
Horsted Keynes	a	10 40	11 40	12 38		13 35	13 55	14 43	15 05	15 52	16 10	16 57	17 15	18 10
Horsted Keynes	d	11 00	11 55	12 50	13 05	13 57	14 12	15 07	15 22	16 12	16 26	17 17	17 32	18 30
Sheffield Park	a	11 13	12 08	13 03	13 18	14 10	14 25	15 20	15 35	16 25	16 39	17 30	17 45	18 43

Saturdays, off-peak Sundays and Good Friday
Saturdays 1 March to 25 October inclusive
Sundays 2 to 30 March inclusive. Also 13 April to 18 May inclusive and 5 to 26 October inclusive
Good Friday, 4 April

		A		A			A	F
Sheffield Park	d	11 40	12 40	13 40	14 50	15 55	17 00	17 55
Horsted Keynes	a	11 55	12 55	13 55	15 05	16 10	17 15	18 10
Horsted Keynes	d	12 10	13 10	14 15	15 22	16 26	17 32	18 25
Sheffield Park	a	12 23	13 23	14 28	15 35	16 39	17 45	18 38

Mid-Week
Tuesdays 7 April to Friday 10 April inclusive
Wednesdays in May and October
Mondays to Fridays, 27 May to 26 September inclusive

		B		G			C	D
Sheffield Park	d	11 40	12 40	13 40	14 50	15 55	17 00	17 55
Horsted Keynes	a	11 55	12 55	13 55	15 05	16 10	17 15	18 10
Horsted Keynes	d	12 10	13 10	14 10	15 22	16 26	17 31	18 25
Sheffield Park	a	12 23	13 23	14 23	15 35	16 39	17 44	18 38

Winter
Sundays in January and February
Saturdays and Sundays in November
Sundays in December
Boxing Day 26 December (see leaflet for Christmas attractions)
New Year's Day

Sheffield Park	d	12 40	14 50	15 55
Horsted Keynes	a	12 55	15 05	16 10
Horsted Keynes	d	13 10	15 22	16 26
Sheffield Park	a	13 23	15 35	16 39

A Does not run Saturdays in March and October
B Runs weekdays only 27 to 30 May inclusive and 23 June to 29 August inclusive
C Runs weekdays only 21 July to 29 August and on other days for parties or if sufficient demand
D Runs weekdays for pre-arranged party traffic only
E Does not stop at Freshfield Halt
F Runs Saturdays 3 May to 30 August and Sundays 13 April to 18 May
G Runs weekdays only 28 July to 29 August inclusive

Passenger trains stop at Freshfield Halt if required unless otherwise shown
Passengers wishing to entrain must give a clear signal to the driver
Passenger wishing to alight must notify the Guard before boarding the train

Goods Train

These will be run as a public attraction on some Sundays at 10.42 from Sheffield Park

Isle of Wight Steam Railway
Operated by steam traction

6-7 April, 5/26 May, 25 August *Daily week commencing 18 August*
Sundays 4 May to 28 September
Thursdays 3 July to 28 August

												A
Haven Street	d	11 05	11 35	12 05	13 35	14 05	14 35	15 05	15 35	16 05	16 35	17 05
Wootton†												
Haven Street	a	11 25	11 55	12 25	13 55	14 25	14 55	15 25	15 55	16 25	16 55	17 25

A Operates only during July and August
† Trains operate a return trip Haven Street-Wootton-Haven Street. Passengers may not alight at Wootton. All passengers should travel from Haven Street

A reduced service will operate during 18-22 August

Buckfastleigh Line — Dart Valley Railway

This service is operated exclusively by The Dart Valley Light Railway Ltd, to whom all enquiries and communications should be addressed at Buckfastleigh Station, Buckfastleigh, Devon. Tel 2338

Sunday 18 May
Daily 25 May to 14 September

				C FSX	B	C FSX
Buckfastleigh	d	11 30	13 45	15 00	15 30	16 00
Staverton Bridge	d	11 45	14 00	15 15	15 45	16 15
Riverside (Totnes)	a†	11 55	14 10	15 25	15 55	16 25
Riverside (Totnes)	d†	12 10	14 25	15 30	16 10	16 35
Staverton Bridge	d	12 20	14 35	15 40	16 20	16 45
Buckfastleigh	a	12 35	14 50	15 55	16 35	17 00

The Company reserves the right to amend or cancel the timetable without notice

Under normal circumstances trains are steam hauled

B 18 May; daily 25 May to 19 July and 29 August to 14 September also Fridays and Saturdays 25 July to 23 August

C 20 July to 28 August

* On 25, 26 May the timetable is suspended and a frequent service operates commencing from Buckfastleigh at 10 30 (steam rally days)

†Although trains run to the outskirts of Totnes at Riverside station there is no access from the town or BR station to the Dart Valley steam trains at Totnes

The Devon General Omnibus Co (Services 188 and 189) operates from Newton Abbot Bus Station to Buckfastleigh; Approx hourly service on weekdays, limited service on Sundays. Journey time approx 45 minutes

The Western National Omnibus Co (Service 115) operates from Paignton (Bus Station, adjacent to railway stations) and Totnes (Station Approach) to Buckfastleigh on weekdays (Limited service on Summer Sundays). Journey time approx 30 minutes

Paignton and Dartmouth Ferry & Kingswear — Dart Valley Railway

This service is operated exclusively by the Dart Valley Light Railway Ltd to whom all enquiries and communications should be addressed at Queens Park Station, Paignton, Devon Tel 555872

Daily 18 May to 29 June and 6 September to and 12 October Sundays 6 July to 31 August

Paignton (Queens Park) ⇄	d	10 15	12 15	14 15	16 15
Goodrington Sands	d	10 20	12 20	14 20	16 20
Churston	d	10 35	12 35	14 35	16 35
Dartmouth Ferry & Kingswear	a	10 50	12 50	14 50	16 50
Dartmouth Ferry & Kingswear	d	11 15	13 15	15 15	17 15
Churston	d	11 35	13 35	15 35	17 30
Goodrington Sands	d	11 45	13 45	15 45	17 40
Paignton (Queens Park) ⇄	a	11 50	13 50	15 50	17 45

Saturdays 5 July to 30 August

Paignton (Queens Park) ⇄	10 15	12 15	14 15	15 15	17 15
Goodrington Sands	10 20	12 20	14 20	15 20	17 20
Churston	10 30	12 30	14 30	15 30	17 30
Dartmouth Ferry & Kingswear	10 45	12 45		15 45	
Dartmouth Ferry & Kingswear	11 00	13 00		16 00	
Churston	11 15	13 15	14 40	16 15	17 40
Goodrington Sands	11 25	13 25	14 50	16 25	17 50
Paignton (Queens Park) ⇄	11 30	13 30	14 55	16 30	17 55

Mondays to Fridays 30 June to 5 September

					A
Paignton (Queens Park) ⇄	10 15	and	15 15	16 15	17 15
Goodrington Sands	10 20	every	15 20	16 20	17 20
Churston	10 35	hour	15 35	16 35	17 35
Dartmouth Ferry & Kingswear	10 50	until	15 50	16 50	17 50
					A
Dartmouth Ferry & Kingswear	11 15	and	16 15	17 15	18 15
Churston	11 35	every	16 35	17 30	18 30
Goodrington Sands	11 45	hour	16 45	17 40	18 40
Paignton (Queens Park) ⇄	11 50	until	16 50	17 45	18 45

The company reserves the right to amend or cancel the timetable without notice

Under normal circumstances Monday to Friday and Sunday trains are steam hauled

⇄ Adjacent to BR station

†Dartmouth is linked to Dartmouth Ferry & Kingswear station by a ferry service. Although the crossing takes only a few minutes passengers from Dartmouth are advised to allow approx 30 minutes to ensure connection with the train

A Tuesdays, Wednesdays and Thursdays 22 July to 28 August

Llanberis Gilfach Ddu and Cei Llydan — via Penllyn
Cei Llydan and Llanberis Gilfach Ddu — Direct
Llanberis Lake Railway
Rheilffordd Llyn Padarn

Operated by Steam Traction

This service is operated exclusively by Rheilffordd Llyn Padarn Cyf to whom all enquiries and communications should be addressed at Llanberis, Gwynedd LL55 4TY (Tel: Llanberis (028 682) 549

Mondays to Thursdays
22 May to 2 October

		A	A	A
Llanberis Gilfach Ddu	d	13 00	14 00	15 00
Cei Llydan	a	13 23	14 23	15 23
	d	13 30	14 30	15 30
Llanberis Gilfach Ddu	a	13 40	14 40	15 40

Until 21 May

		B	C	B	C		B	C	B		B	C	B		B	C	B	D	B
Llanberis Gilfach Ddu	d	10 30	11 00	11 30	11 45	12 30	13 00	13 15	13 30	14 00	14 30	14 45	15 00	15 30	16 00	16 15	16 45	17 00	17 30
Cei Llydan	a	10 53	11 23	11 53	12 08	12 53	13 23	13 38	13 53	14 23	14 53	15 08	15 23	15 53	16 23	16 38	17 08	17 23	17 53
	d	11 00	11 30	12 00	12 15	13 00	13 30	13 45	14 00	14 30	15 00	15 15	15 30	16 00	16 30	16 45	17 15	17 30	18 00
Llanberis Gilfach Ddu	a	11 10	11 40	12 10	12 25	13 10	13 40	13 55	14 10	14 40	15 10	15 25	15 40	16 10	16 40	16 55	17 25	17 40	18 10

Sunday 18 May

Llanberis Gilfach Ddu	d	13 00	14 00	15 00
Cei Llydan	a	13 23	14 23	15 23
	d	13 30	14 30	15 30
Llanberis Gilfach Ddu	a	13 40	14 40	15 40

Fridays, Saturdays and Sundays
23 May to 5 October

							E
Llanberis Gilfach Ddu	d	13 00	14 00	14 45	15 30	16 15	17 00
Cei Llydan	a	13 23	14 23	15 08	15 53	16 38	17 23
	d	13 30	14 30	15 15	16 00	16 45	17 30
Llanberis Gilfach Ddu	a	13 40	14 40	15 25	16 10	16 55	17 40

A Not Thursday 15 May
B 22 May to 29 May and 30 June to 28 August
C 2 June to 26 June and 1 September to 2 October
D 2 June to 26 June
E 4 July to 24 August

Passengers will not be picked up or put down at Penllyn

Llanberis and Snowdon Summit — Snowdon Mountain Railway

Operated by Steam Traction

This service is operated exclusively by the Snowdon Mountain Railway Company Ltd to whom all enquiries should be addressed at Llanberis, Gwynedd. Tel: Llanberis 223

Mondays to Fridays Until 3 October, Saturdays and Sundays, 24, 25 May and 12 July to 7 September

Trains will not leave the terminus for the ascent with less than 25 return passengers or the equivalent in adult fares if the Company so determines.

Llanberis	d	09 00	Thereafter at half-hourly intervals,	Last train departs	18 30 until 12 Sept
Snowdon Summit	d	10 30	weather and traffic permitting	Snowdon Summit	17 00 from 13 Sept

Snow and ice may prevent progress to summit early and late in the season and strong winds at any time

All other Saturdays and Sundays until 14 September

09 30	Reduced service depending upon demand
11 00	weather and traffic permitting

Porthmadog and Tanygrisiau — Festiniog Railway

This service is operated exclusively by the Festiniog Railway Co Ltd to whom all enquiries should be addressed at Harbour Station, Porthmadog, Gwynedd

Mondays to Saturdays and Sundays until 18 May and 21 September to 31 October

Porthmadog	d	10 00	12 30	15 00
Minffordd	d	10 08	12 38	15 08
Penrhyn	d	10 15	12 45	15 15
Tan-y-Bwlch	d	10 36	13 06	15 36
Tanygrisiau	d	11 00	13 30	16 00
Blaenau Ffestiniog†	a			
Blaenau Ffestiniog†	d			
Tanygrisiau	d	11 10	13 40	16 10
Tan-y-Bwlch	d	11 30	14 00	16 30
Penrhyn	d	11 45	14 15	16 45
Minffordd	d	11 50	14 20	16 50
Porthmadog	a	12 04	14 34	17 04

Mondays to Fridays 19 May to 23 May 2 June to 11 July and 1 September to 19 September

Porthmadog	d	10 00	11 00	12 00	13 00	14 00	15 00	16 00
Minffordd	d	10 08	11 08	12 08	13 08	14 08	15 08	16 08
Penrhyn	d	10 15	11 15	12 15	13 15	14 15	15 15	16 15
Tan-y-Bwlch	d	10 36	11 36	12 36	13 36	14 36	15 36	16 36
Tanygrisiau	d	11 02	12 02	13 02	14 02	15 02	16 02	17 02
Blaenau Ffestiniog†	a							
Blaenau Ffestiniog†	d							
Tanygrisiau	d	11 40	12 40	13 40	14 40	15 40	16 40	17 10
Tan-y-Bwlch	d	12 05	13 05	14 05	15 05	16 05	17 05	17 30
Penrhyn	d	12 22	13 22	14 22	15 22	16 22	17 20	17 45
Minffordd	d	12 30	13 30	14 30	15 30	16 30	17 25	17 50
Porthmadog	a	12 44	13 44	14 44	15 44	16 44	17 39	18 04

Saturdays and Sundays 31 May to 6 July and 6 September to 20 September

Porthmadog	d	10 00	12 30	15 00
Minffordd	d	10 08	12 38	15 08
Penrhyn	d	10 15	12 45	15 15
Tan-y-Bwlch	d	10 36	13 06	15 36
Tanygrisiau	d	11 00	13 30	16 00
Blaenau Ffestiniog†	a			
Blaenau Ffestiniog†	d			
Tanygrisiau	d	11 10	13 40	16 40
Tan-y-Bwlch	d	11 30	14 00	17 00
Penrhyn	d	11 45	14 15	17 15
Minffordd	d	11 50	14 20	17 20
Porthmadog	a	12 04	14 34	17 34

1 November to 22 March (see note A)

Porthmadog	d	11 30	14 30
Minffordd	d	11 38	14 38
Penrhyn	d	11 45	14 45
Tan-y-Bwlch	d	12 06	15 06
Tanygrisiau	d	12 30	15 30
Blaenau Ffestiniog†	a		
Blaenau Ffestiniog†	d		
Tanygrisiau	d	13 10	15 40
Tan-y-Bwlch	d	13 30	16 00
Penrhyn	d	13 45	16 15
Minffordd	d	13 50	16 20
Porthmadog	a	14 04	16 34

Mondays to Fridays 26 May to 30 May and 14 July to 29 August

		FX									FX	FX		FX	FX
Porthmadog	d	09 00	09 40	10 10	11 00	11 30	12 00	12 30	13 25	13 55	14 25	14 55	15 50	16 20	16 50
Minffordd	d		09 48	10 18	11 08	11 38	12 08	12 38	13 33	14 03	14 33	15 03	15 58	16 28	16 58
Penrhyn	d		09 55	10 25	11 15	11 45	12 15	12 45	13 40	14 10	14 40	15 10	16 05	16 35	17 05
Tan-y-Bwlch	d		10 18	10 48	11 38	12 08	12 38	13 08	14 03	14 33	15 03	15 33	16 28	16 58	17 28
Tanygrisiau	d	09 56	10 37	11 12	12 00	12 31	13 01	13 31	14 22	14 56	15 26	15 56	16 47	17 17	17 47
Blaenau Ffestiniog	a														
		FX									FX			FX	FX
Blaenau Ffestiniog†	d														
Tanygrisiau	d	10 15	10 50	11 20	12 10	12 40	13 10	13 40	14 35	15 05	15 35	16 05	16 55	17 25	17 55
Tan-y-Bwlch	d	12 45	11 10	11 40	12 35	13 05	13 30	14 00	15 00	15 30	15 55	16 25	17 25	17 50	18 15
Penrhyn	d	11 00	11 30	12 00	13 00	13 25	13 55	14 25	15 25	15 50	16 20	16 50	17 40	18 05	18 35
Minffordd	d	11 10	11 40	12 10	13 05	13 35	14 05	14 35	15 30	16 00	16 30	17 00	17 45	18 10	18 40
Porthmadog	a	11 20	11 50	12 20	13 15	13 44	14 14	14 44	15 40	16 09	16 39	17 09	17 58	18 24	18 50

Saturdays and Sundays 24 and 25 May and 12 July to 31 August

		FX								
Porthmadog	d	19 00	10 00	11 00	12 00	13 00	14 00	15 00	16 00	19 00
Minffordd	d	19 08	10 08	11 08	12 08	13 08	14 08	15 08	16 08	19 08
Penrhyn	d	19 15	10 15	11 15	12 15	13 15	14 15	15 15	16 15	19 15
Tan-y-Bwlch	d	19 36	10 36	11 36	12 36	13 36	14 36	15 36	16 36	19 36
Tanygrisiau	d	20 00	11 02	12 02	13 02	14 02	15 02	16 02	17 02	20 00
Blaenau Ffestiniog	a									
		FX								
Blaenau Ffestiniog	d									
Tanygrisiau	d	20 10	11 40	12 40	13 40	14 40	15 40	16 40	17 10	20 10
Tan-y-Bwlch	d	20 30	12 05	13 05	14 05	15 05	16 05	17 05	17 30	20 30
Penrhyn	d	20 45	12 22	13 22	14 22	15 22	16 22	17 20	17 45	20 45
Minffordd	d	20 50	12 30	13 30	14 30	15 30	16 30	17 25	17 50	20 50
Porthmadog	a	21 04	12 44	13 44	14 44	15 44	16 44	17 39	18 04	21 04

†connecting bus service (see local announcements)

A Saturdays and Sundays 1, 2, 8, 9 November, 20, 21 December, Mondays to Satrudays and Sundays 26 December to 1 January, Saturdays and Sundays 14 February to 22 March

Tywyn, Abergynolwyn and Nant Gwernol — Talyllyn Railway

Operated by Steam Traction

This service is operated exclusively by the Talyllyn Railway Company to whom all enquiries and communications should be addressed at Wharf Station, Tywyn, Gwynedd LL36 9EY

Tywyn Wharf station is 300 yards from Tywyn BR station

		Daily to 16 May	*Mondays to Fridays 19 to 23 May 2 to 13 June 1 to 26 Sept*			*Sats 17 May 31 May, 7 June 6 to 27 Sept*	*Sundays 18 May, 1, 8 June, 7, 28 Sept*		*24 May to 30 May and 14 June to 11 July Mondays to Fridays*						*Saturdays and Sundays*	
			C													
Tywyn Wharf	d	14 30	10 00	12 30	14 50	14 30	12 30	14 50	10 00	11 20	12 20	13 50	14 50	16 15	12 20	14 50
Dolgoch Falls	d	15 00	10 30	13 00	15 20	15 00	13 00	15 20	10 30	11 50	12 50	14 20	15 20	16 45	12 50	15 20
Abergynolwyn	d	15 15	10 45	13 15	15 35	15 15	13 15	15 35	10 45	12 10	13 10	14 40	15 40	17 15	13 10	15 40
Nant Gwernol	a	15 24	10 54	13 24	15 44	15 24	13 24	15 44	10 54	12 16	13 16	14 46	15 46	17 21	13 16	15 46
			C													
Nant Gwernol	d	15 30	11 00	13 30	15 50	15 30	13 30	15 50	11 00	12 22	13 22	14 52	15 52	17 27	13 22	15 52
Abergynolwyn	a	15 36	11 06	13 36	15 56	15 36	13 36	15 56	11 06	12 28	13 28	14 58	15 58	17 33	13 28	15 58
	d	15 55	11 15	13 55	16 10	15 55	13 55	16 10	11 15	12 50	13 45	15 20	16 10	17 35	13 45	16 10
Dolgoch Falls	d	16 10	11 30	14 10	16 25	16 10	14 10	16 25	11 30	13 05	14 00	15 35	16 25	17 50	14 00	16 25
Tywyn Wharf	a	16 37	11 57	14 37	16 51	16 37	14 37	16 51	11 58	13 33	14 30	16 03	16 54	18 18	14 28	16 52

		Mondays to Fridays 12 July to 31 August Saturdays and Sundays											*30 Sept to 2 Nov*						
												A WO						B	MFX
Tywyn Wharf	d	09 50	10 25	11 00	11 50	12 40	13 30	14 20	15 10	16 00	16 50	19 20	11 20	12 20	13 50	14 50	16 15	19 20	14 30
Dolgoch Falls	d	10 20	10 55	11 35	12 25	13 15	14 05	14 55	15 45	16 35	17 25	19 50	11 50	12 50	14 20	15 20	16 45	19 50	15 00
Abergynolwyn	d	10 34	11 15	11 50	12 40	13 30	14 20	15 10	16 00	16 50	17 45	20 05	12 10	13 10	14 40	15 40	17 15	20 05	15 15
Nant Gwernol	a	10 42	11 21	11 56	12 46	13 36	14 26	15 16	16 06	16 56	17 51	20 11	12 16	13 16	14 46	15 46	17 21	20 11	15 24
												A WO						B	MFX
Nant Gwernol	d	10 48	11 30	12 05	12 55	13 45	14 35	15 25	16 15	17 05	17 55	20 18	12 22	13 22	14 52	15 52	17 27	20 18	15 30
Abergynolwyn	a	10 54	11 36	12 11	13 01	13 51	14 41	15 31	16 21	17 11	18 01	20 24	12 28	13 28	14 58	15 58	17 33	20 24	15 36
	d	10 58	11 50	12 40	13 30	14 20	15 10	16 00	16 50	17 40	18 05	20 45	12 50	13 45	15 20	16 10	17 35	20 45	15 55
Dolgoch Falls	d	11 10	12 00	12 50	13 40	14 30	15 20	16 10	17 00	17 50	18 15	20 00	13 05	14 00	15 35	16 25	17 50	21 00	16 10
Tywyn Wharf	a	11 39	12 29	13 19	14 09	14 59	15 49	16 39	17 29	18 19	18 45	21 25	13 33	14 30	16 03	16 54	18 18	21 25	16 37

For details of Christmas and Easter train services, see local announcements

Trains also stop as required at Tywyn Pendre, Hendy, Fach Goch, Cynfal, Rhydyronen, Tynyllwynhen, Brynglas and Quarry Siding. Passengers wishing to alight must give notice at the time of booking. Passengers desiring to join must give an appropriate hand signal to the driver

A 16 July to 27 August
B Sundays only 20 July to 24 August
C Until 19 September

Llanfair Caereinion and Sylfaen — Welshpool and Llanfair Light Railway

Operated by Steam Traction

Saturdays and Sundays, 3 May to 5 October,
Mondays to Fridays 26 May to 30 May and
16 June to 5 September

This service is operated exclusively by the Welshpool and Llanfair Light Railway Preservation Co Ltd, to whom all enquiries and communications should be addressed at Llanfair Station, Llanfair Caereinion, Powys. Tel: 441

One Class Only

		A		B
Llanfair Caereinion	d	11 15	14 15	16 15
Heniarth	d			
Cyfronydd	d			
Castle Caereinion	a	11 45	14 45	16 45
Sylfaen	a	11 55	14 55	16 55

Sylfaen	d	12 05	15 10	17 05
Castle Caereinion	d	12 15	15 20	17 15
Cyfronydd	d			
Heniarth	d			
Llanfair Caereinion	a	12 50	15 55	17 50

Service to Welshpool (Raven Square) temporarily suspended

A Daily 24 May to 1 June and 14 June to 7 September except Mondays 16 June to 18 August and 1 September
B Not Tuesdays to Fridays 17 June to 18 July and 2 to 5 September

Extra trains will run as required at Bank Holiday periods

Services will also operate during Easter and Spring 1981. For details apply direct to the Welshpool and Llanfair Light Railway Preservation Co Ltd at the address shown above

Sheringham and Weybourne — North Norfolk Railway

Operated by Steam Traction

This service is operated exclusively by the North Norfolk Railway Company Limited to whom all communications should be addressed at Sheringham Station, Sheringham, Norfolk NR26 8RA. Telephone Sheringham 822045

Sundays until 19 October
All Bank Holiday Mondays
Tuesdays and Thursdays 22 July to 4 September
Saturdays 28 June to 27 September

		A SX	B			A
Sheringham	d	11 45	12 50	14 00	15 20	16 45
Weybourne	a	12 00	13 05	14 15	15 35	17 00
Weybourne	d	12 15	13 20	14 30	15 50	17 10
Sheringham	a	12 30	13 35	14 45	16 05	17 25

Additional trains will be run at peak periods and will be advertised locally

For details of Christmas special trains see local announcements

A These trains may be operated by Diesel Railbus in early and late season
B Runs Wednesdays and Bank Holiday Mondays; also Sundays 27 July to 7 September

The Company reserves the right to cancel, alter, or suspend trains and accept no liability for any loss, inconvenience or delay thereby caused

Wansford and Orton Mere— Nene Valley Railway

4 April to 12 October

			*	*	*	*	
		BD	BCD	ACD	AC	A	B
Wansford	d	11 15	12 30	14 00	15 10	16 20	17 20
Ferry Meadows	d	11 30	12 45	14 15	15 25	16 35	17 35
Orton Mere	a	11 35	12 50	14 20	15 30	16 40	17 40

			*	*	*	*	
		BD	BCD	ACD	AC	A	B
Orton Mere	d	11 45	13 00	14 30	15 40	16 50	17 50
Ferry Meadows	d	11 50	13 05	14 35	15 45	16 55	17 55
Wansford	a	12 05	13 20	14 50	16 00	17 10	18 10

A Saturdays, Sundays and Bank Holidays 4 April-28 September
B Sundays 25 May-24 August also Sundays 6 April and 4 May and Mondays 7 April & 26 May and 25 August
C Tuesdays, Wednesdays and Thursdays in July and August
D Wednesdays and Thursdays during June

'Scandia' or 'Greene King' Bar on all trains Sundays and Bank Holidays
*Wagons-Lits restaurant car serving lunch and afternoon teas on Sundays and Bank Holidays

'EUROSTEAM 80' enthusiasts weekend 20/21 September. Special service in operation. Please enquire for details.

Loughborough and Rothley — Great Central Railway
Operated by Steam Traction

This service is operated exclusively by the Great Central Railway Company (1976) to whom all communications should be addressed at Great Central Station, PO Box 33, Loughborough, Leics LE11 1SS

Refreshment facilities are available at Loughborough Central and Rothley stations

Wednesdays and Thursdays
2 July to 28 August

					A
Loughborough Central	d	14 30	15 45	17 00	19 30
Quorn & Woodhouse	a	14 38	15 53	17 08	19 38
	d	14 40	15 55	17 10	19 40
Rothley	a	14 51	16 06	17 21	19 51

					A
Rothley	d	15 05	16 20	17 35	20 40
Quorn & Woodhouse	a	15 16	16 31	17 46	20 51
	d	15 18	16 33	17 48	20 52
Loughborough Central	a	15 26	16 41	15 56	21 00

Saturdays and Sundays

C	C			D	E
11 45	13 15	14 45	16 00	17 15	19 30
11 53	13 23	14 53	16 08	17 23	
11 55	13 25	14 55	16 10	17 25	
12 06	13 36	15 06	16 21	17 36	20 20

B	C				D	E
11 00	12 20	13 55	15 20	16 35	17 50	20 40
11 11	12 31	14 06	15 31	16 46	18 01	
11 13	12 33	14 08	15 33	16 48	18 03	
11 21	12 41	14 16	15 41	16 56	18 11	21 00

Buffet facilities available on all trains

Trains will also run at Bank Holiday periods except Christmas Day and Good Friday

The Company reserves the right to deviate from or suspend the above Timetable subject to operational considerations

A Available for parties booked in advance
B Sundays only
C Luncheon service available
D Saturdays only until 28 September
E Special Dinner service

Bridgnorth and Bewdley — Severn Valley Railway
Operated by Steam Traction

First and Third Class

This service is operated exclusively by the Severn Valley Railway Company Ltd to whom all enquiries and communications should be addressed at The Railway Station Bewdley, Worcs Tel: 403816

Mondays to Fridays
14 July to 3 September
(Services A & B operate before this period.
See relevant footnotes for actual dates)
Saturdays
Until 25 October

		B	A		B		A			
Bridgnorth	d	10 15	11 20	12 05	12 45	13 35	14 20	15 05	16 35	18 05
Eardington	d							Q		
Hampton Loade	d		11 39	12 24		13 54	14 39	15 24	16 54	18 24
Highley	d		11 49	12 34		14 04	14 49	15 34	17 04	18 34
Arley	d		12 01	12 46		14 14	15 01	15 44	17 14	18 44
Northwood	d		x	x		x	x	x	x	x
Bewdley	a	10 58	12 15	13 00	13 28	14 30	15 15	16 00	17 30	18 58
Foley Park	a									

		B		A		B		A		
Foley Park	d									
Bewdley	d	11 30	11 45	12 30	13 15	14 00	14 45	15 30	16 15	17 45
Northwood	d		x	x	x		x	x	x	x
Arley	d		12 03	12 48	13 33		15 03	15 48	16 33	18 03
Highley	d		12 13	12 58	13 43		15 13	15 58	16 43	18 13
Hampton Loade	d		12 15	13 06	13 55		15 25	16 08	16 55	18 25
Eardington	d		Q							
Bridgnorth	a	12 13	12 40	13 23	14 10	14 43	15 40	16 23	17 10	18 40

Sundays
Until 26 October
Also operates on Mondays 26 May and 25 August
and Tuesdays 27 May and 24 August

	D		E		D		E		E	
Bridgnorth	11 20	12 05	12 50	13 35	14 20	15 05	15 50	16 35	17 20	18 05
Eardington										
Hampton Loade	11 39	12 24	13 09	13 54	14 39	15 24	16 09	16 54	17 39	18 24
Highley	11 49	12 34	13 19	14 04	14 49	15 34	16 19	17 04	17 49	18 34
Arley	12 01	12 46	13 31	14 16	15 01	15 46	16 31	17 16	18 01	18 44
Northwood	x	x	x	x	x	x	x	x	x	x
Bewdley	12 15	13 00	13 45	14 30	15 15	16 00	16 45	17 30	18 15	18 58
Foley Park										

	E		D		E		D		E	
Foley Park										
Bewdley	11 00	11 45	12 30	13 15	14 00	14 45	15 30	16 15	17 00	17 45
Northwood	x	x	x	x	x	x	x	x	x	x
Arley	11 18	12 03	12 48	13 33	14 18	15 03	15 48	16 33	17 10	18 03
Highley	11 28	12 13	12 58	13 43	14 20	15 13	15 58	16 43	17 28	18 13
Hampton Loade	11 40	12 25	13 10	13 55	14 40	15 25	16 10	16 55	17 40	18 25
Eardington										
Bridgnorth	11 55	12 40	13 25	14 10	14 55	15 40	16 25	17 10	17 55	18 40

Whilst every effort will be made to maintain the above service, the Company do not guarantee that the trains will depart or arrive at the times stated and reserve the right to cancel, alter or suspend, any train without notice and accept no liability for any loss, inconvenience or delay thereby caused. The Company accept no liability for any in accuracy in the information contained herewith.
All trains are steam hauled under normal circumstances

A May 28, 29 and 30 only
B Tuesdays, Wednesdays and Thursdays only 20 to 22 May and 3 June to 10 July
Q Stops on request on Saturdays only

A special intensive service operates on Saturdays 14, 28 June, 6 September and 11 October and Sundays 15, 29 June, 7 September and 12 October

Sundays
D Until 14 September
E 29 June to 14 September

Grosmont and Pickering — North York Moors Railway

Monday to Friday
1 April to 23 May (NOT 7 April or 5 May — see Table 3)
1 September to 31 October
Saturdays 12 April to 17 May; 13 September to 1 November (Not 3 May)
National Park Diesel Scenic Service

Grosmont	d	11 00	13 00	15 00	16 45
Goathland	a	11 10	13 10	15 10	16 55
Goathland	d	11 15	13 15	15 15	16 55A
Levisham	d	11 40	13 40	15 40	17 30
Pickering	a	12 00	14 00	16 00	17 50

Pickering	d	10 30	12 30	14 30	16 10
Levisham	d	10 50	12 50	14 50	16 30
Goathland	a	11 14	13 14	15 14	16 54A
Goathland	d	11 15	13 15	15 15	17 05
Grosmont	a	11 25	13 25	15 25	17 15

Monday to, Friday 27 May to 25 July
Saturday 5 April 3, 24 May to 6 September
Sunday 13 April to 18 May, 14 September to 2 November

		D	Z	Y	Y	Z	Y	Y	D	D	THU D	THU D
Grosmont	d	09 50	11 00	12 00	13 00	14 00	15 00	16 00	17 00	18 00	19 05	20 20
Goathland	a	10 05	11 15	12 15	13 15	14 15	15 15	16 15	17 15	18 15	19 14	20 30
Goathland	d	10 18	11 18	12 18	13 18	14 18	15 18	16 18	17 18	18 18	19 15	20 35
Levisham	a	10 42	11 42	12 42	13 42	14 42	15 42	16 42	17 42	18 42	19 40	21 00
Levisham	d	10 45	11 45	12 45	13 45	14 45	15 45	16 45	17 45	18 45	19 41	21 01
Pickering	a	11 05	12 05	13 05	14 05	15 05	16 05	17 05	18 05	19 05	20 00	21 20

		D	Y	Y	Z	Y	Y	Z	D	D	THU D	THU D
Pickering	d	09 10	10 20	11 20	12 20	13 20	14 20	15 20	16 20	17 20	19 20	20 40
Levisham	a	09 30	10 40	11 40	12 40	13 40	14 40	15 40	16 40	17 40	19 39	20 59
Levisham	d	09 34	10 44	11 44	12 44	13 44	14 44	15 44	16 44	17 44	19 40	21 00
Goathland	a	10 01	11 11	12 11	13 11	14 11	15 11	16 11	17 11	18 11	20 04	21 24
Goathland	d	10 10	11 20	12 20	13 20	14 20	15 20	16 20	17 20	18 20	20 05	21 25
Grosmont	a	10 20	11 30	12 30	13 30	14 30	15 30	16 30	17 30	18 30	20 15	21 35

Monday to Friday 28 July to 29 August
Saturdays (see Table 2)
Sunday 6 April & 25 May to 7 September
Bank Holidays 7 April, 5, 26 May

		S	S	D	S	S	D	S	D	D	THU D	THU D
Grosmont	d	09 50	11 00	12 00	13 00	14 00	15 00	16 00	17 00	18 00	19 05	20 20
Goathland	a	10 05	11 15	12 15	13 15	14 15	15 15	16 15	17 15	18 15	19 14	20 30
Goathland	d	10 18	11 18	12 18	13 18	14 18	15 18	16 18	17 18	18 18	19 15	20 35
Levisham	a	10 42	11 42	12 42	13 42	14 42	15 42	16 42	17 42	18 42	19 40	21 00
Levisham	d	10 45	11 45	12 45	13 45	14 45	15 45	16 45	17 45	18 45	19 41	21 01
Pickering	a	11 05	12 05	13 05	14 05	15 05	16 05	17 05	18 05	19 05	20 00	21 20

		D	D	S	S	D	S	S	D	S	THU D	THU D
Pickering	d	09 10	10 20	11 20	12 20	13 20	14 20	15 20	16 20	17 20	19 20	20 40
Levisham	a	09 30	10 40	11 40	12 40	13 40	14 40	15 40	16 40	17 40	19 39	20 59
Levisham	d	09 34	10 44	11 44	12 44	13 44	14 44	15 44	16 44	17 44	19 40	21 00
Goathland	a	10 01	11 11	12 11	13 11	14 11	15 11	16 11	17 11	18 11	20 04	21 24
Goathland	d	10 10	11 20	12 20	13 20	14 20	15 20	16 20	17 20	18 20	20 05	21 25
Grosmont	a	10 20	11 30	12 30	13 30	14 30	15 30	16 30	17 30	18 30	20 15	21 35

S Steam throughout
D Diesel throughout
Y Monday-Friday
Diesel Pickering-Goathland/Steam Goathland-Grosmont
Saturday & Sunday
Z Diesel throughout
Monday-Friday
Diesel Pickering-Goathland/Steam Goathland-Grosmont
Saturday & Sunday
Steam throughout
THU-Thursdays only in July and August
A Change at Goathland

British Rail trains arrive and depart from platform 1 at Grosmont, the Moorsrail booking office is on platform 2 and Moorsrail trains normally arrive and depart from platform 3

High fire risk or other circumstances may require a change of motive power without prior notice

Ticket issued subject to regulations

Ravenglass and Dalegarth — Ravenglass and Eskdale Railway

This service is operated exclusively by the Ravenglass and Eskdale Railway Company Limited, to whom all enquiries and communications should be addressed at Ravenglass, Cumbria CA18 1SW.
Tel. Ravenglass (06577) 226

Mondays to Saturdays and Sundays until 24 May and 8 September to 26 October

		A	A	B	A		A	B	A
Ravenglass	d	09 20	11 35	12 05	12 35	14 35	15 35	16 40	16 50
Muncaster Mill	d								
Irton Road	d	09 40	11 55	12 25	12 55	14 55	15 55	17 00	17 10
The Green	d	09 45	12 00	12 30	13 00	15 00	16 00	17 05	17 15
Beckfoot	d	s	s	s	s	s	s	s	s
Eskdale (Dalegarth)	a	10 00	12 25	12 45	13 15	15 15	16 15	17 20	17 25

		H	J	A			A
Eskdale (Dalegarth)	d	07 45	10 20	12 35	13 35	15 35	16 35
Beckfoot	d	07 48	10 23	u	u	u	u
The Green	d	07 52	10 32	12 47	13 47	15 47	16 45
Irton Road	d	08 00	10 40	12 55	13 55	15 55	16 50
Muncaster Mill	d						
Ravenglass	a	08 20	11 00	13 15	14 15	16 15	17 15

Mondays to Saturdays and Sundays 25 May to 7 September

				C		C		D		D		D		D			E
Ravenglass	d	09 20	10 35	11 05	11 35	12 05	12 35	13 05	13 35	14 05	14 35	15 05	15 35	16 05	16 50	17 50	18 45
Muncester Mill	d																
Irton Road	d	09 40	10 55	11 25	11 55	12 25	12 55	13 25	13 55	14 25	14 55	15 25	15 55	16 25	17 10	18 10	19 05
The Green	d	09 45	11 00	11 30	12 00	12 30	13 00	13 30	14 00	14 30	15 00	15 30	16 00	16 30	17 15	18 15	19 10
Beckfoot	d	s	s	s	s	s	s	s	s	s	s	s	s	s	s	s	s
Eskdale (Dalegarth)	a	10 00	11 25	11 55	12 25	12 55	13 25	13 55	14 25	14 55	15 25	15 55	16 25	16 55	17 30	18 30	19 25

					C		C		D		D		D		D		E
Eskdlae (Dalegarth)	d	07 45	10 20	11 35	12 05	12 35	13 05	13 35	14 05	14 35	15 05	15 35	16 05	16 35	17 10	17 50	18 45
Beckfoot	d	07 48	10 23	u	u	u	u	u	u	u	u	u	u	u	u	u	u
The Green	d	07 52	10 32	11 47	12 17	12 47	13 17	13 47	14 17	14 47	15 17	15 47	16 17	16 45	17 17	18 02	18 57
Irton Road	d	08 00	10 40	11 55	12 25	12 55	13 25	13 55	14 25	14 55	15 25	15 55	16 25	16 50	17 25	18 10	19 05
Muncester Mill	d																
Ravenglass	a	08 20	11 00	12 25	12 55	13 25	13 55	14b25	14 55	15 25	15 55	16b25	16 50	17 15	17 45	18 30	19 25

This timetable is subject to alteration without notice

Additional trains will operate at busy periods

A Until 28 September
B 29 September to 26 October
C 14 July to 28 August. Not Fridays, Saturdays and Sundays
D 13 July to 31 August. Not Fridays, and Saturdays
E 13 July to 31 August
G Mondays to Fridays 27 October to 19 December and from 5 January
H Mondays to Fridays only from 29 September
J Saturdays and Sundays only from 4 October
b Arrives 10 minutes earlier until 12 July
s Trains stop on request to the Guard to set down only
u Trains stop on request to pick up only
The terminus at Ravenglass adjoins British Rail's Ravenglass station

Lakeside and Haverthwaite Railway

Operated by Steam Traction

One Class Only

**This service is operated exclusively by the Lakeside and Haverthwaite Railway Co, Ltd to whom all enquiries and communications should be addressed at Haverthwaite Station, Ulverston, Cumbria LA12 8AL.
Tel. Newby Bridge (04483) 594**

Mondays to Fridays 19 May to 12 September
Sundays 18 May to 14 September

		A						B
Haverthwaite	d	11 10	12 35	13 25	14 35	15 35	16 25	17 35
Newby Bridge	d	11 21	12 45	13 35	14 48	15 48	16 35	17 45
Lakeside	a	11 28	12 50	13 40	14 53	15 53	16 40	17 50
Windermere Sailings	d	*11 40*		*13 45*	*15 15*		*16 45*	
								B
Windermere Sailings	a	*11 55*		*13 25*	*14 55*		*16 25*	*17 55*
Lakeside	d	12 05	13 00	13 55	15 10	16 00	16 55	13 05
Newby Bridge	d	12 11	13 06	14 01	15 16	16 06	17 01	13 11
Haverthwaite	a	12 23	13 15	14 12	15 25	16 15	17 12	13 22

Saturdays until 4 October
Mondays to Fridays and Sundays until 16 May and 15 September to 5 October

Haverthwaite	d	11 55	12 55	13 55	14 55	15 45
Newby Bridge	d	12 05	13 05	14 05	15 05	15 55
Lakeside	a	12 10	13 10	14 10	15 10	16 00
Windermere Sailings	d	*12 30*	*13 20*		*15 20*	*16 10*
Windermere Sailings	a	*12 20*	*13 10*		*15 10*	*16 00*
Lakeside	d	12 30	13 20	12 40	15 20	16 15
Newby Bridge	d	12 35	13 25	14 25	15 25	16 20
Haverthwaite	a	12 45	13 35	14 35	15 35	16 30

Sundays 12 to 26 October

Haverthwaite	d	12 00	14 00	15 00
Newby Bridge	d	12 11	14 11	15 11
Lakeside	a	12 18	14 18	15 18
Lakeside	d	12 30	14 30	15 30
Newby Bridge	d	12 36	14 36	15 36
Haverthwaite	a	12 48	14 48	15 48

A service will operate during Easter and early Spring
Additional services may be operated depending on demand

Whilst every effort will be made to maintain the above Service the Company do not guarantee that the trains will depart or arrive at the times stated and reserve the right to cancel, alter or suspend any train without notice and accept no liability for any loss, inconvenience or delay thereby caused
Under normal circumstances the trains are steam hauled. This timetable may be modified on exceptionally busy days, and may be withdrawn or altered without notice at any time. The Company accept no liabilility for any inaccuracy in the information contained in this timetable.
Through bookings to Bowness and Ambleside using trains and Windermere Sailings are available at Haverthwaite, and vice versa

A From 8 September Windermere Sailing dep 12 15
B 25 May to 30 May and 13 July to 7 September

Aviemore and Boat of Garten — Strathspey Railway

Operated by steam traction

This service is operated exclusively by the Strathspey Railway Company Limited, to whom all enquiries and communications should be addressed at The Station, Boat of Garten, Inverness-shire PH24 3BH. Tel 692

Aviemore Speyside station is 600 yards from Aviemore BR station.

Tuesdays, Wednesdays and Thursdays 1 July to 28 August
Saturdays and Sundays 17 May to 19 October

		A SX				
Aviemore (Speyside)	d	10 40	13 20	14 40	16 00	17 20
Boat of Garten	a	11 00	13 40	15 00	16 20	17 40

		A SX	A SX	B Sun	SO			
Boat of Garten	d	10 00	11 20	12 40	12 40	14 00	15 20	16 40
Aviemore (Speyside)	a	10 20	11 40	13 00	13 00	14 20	15 40	17 00

Additional services may be operated depending on demand

A 29 June to 31 August
B Until 22 June and from 7 September